Contact the author:
www.davidhcampbell.com

Contact the publisher:
David Campbell Christian Publishing
trinitycc@rogers.com

Scripture quotations are from the ESV® Bible (The Holy Bible, English Standard Version®), copyright © 2001 by Crossway, a publishing ministry of Good News Publishers. Used by permission. All rights reserved.

ISBN-13:978-1-7773978-0-7

Printed in the United States of America
Ingram Printing & Distribution, 2021

First Edition

NO DIVING

10 WAYS TO AVOID THE SHALLOW

END OF YOUR FAITH AND GO DEEPER

INTO THE BIBLE

DAVID CAMPBELL

TABLE OF CONTENTS

FOREWORD

NATHAN FINOCHIO

Evil genius of Bond-villain proportions — that's what we call David behind his back. I've known him for some twenty plus years now. I knew him first through my Dad's high praise of him, stories being recounted on our way back from a visit to Owen Sound, ON, where David pastored, Dad bursting into laughter over something devilishly witty David had offered over lunch. When David isn't deconstructing dispensationalism or explaining the *parousia*, he's got this mischievous manner about him that is wildly endearing. If he hadn't gone the theological route, he would have made an excellent sketch writer for Monty Python.

I tend to be attracted to people who enjoy throwing

a barbecue at which "sacred cow" is served. It is my conviction that the church world —particularly the charismatic world —is in desperate need of theological clarity. And it takes a person with some courage to butcher the sacred cows. Most people are superstitious. David and I are (to quote The Office) a little-stitious — and I think it takes that to challenge things that are "spiritual."

And this is why this book delivers for millennials especially. Not because it's dumbed down (because it's not); and not because it praises them and tells them how the world is their oyster. This book connects with millennials because they want the truth, and there are a lot of strange doctrinal holdouts that continue to raise questions for them.

Millennials don't want to be padded. They want answers. That's why all our students at TheosU and TheosSeminary will be buying this book. I will also be recommending this book to every young charismatic leader, teacher, and speaker. Because we have to finally square away what faith is, and the type of language we should use to discuss it. We need to understand our eschatology, and not avoid it because it's confusing, but rather run to it because it's what millennials are asking about.

We need to understand worship and the priesthood of

the believer. We need a theology of money. We have to understand the baptism of the Holy Spirit and what normative Christian experience is. We need clear teaching on prophecy that we can trust and build on. We need clarity on the kingdom of God, especially in a time when everyone has their pet definition of it. Perhaps my favorite chapter was on law and grace, a topic that has always been relevant, and is especially applicable to my generation. We need a tried and true Biblical vision of the church, and not just a utilitarian theory developed from "what grows." And we need a fresh shot in the arm to contend for healing — but how do we do that as thinking people?

That's probably been my greatest frustration as a charismatic. How should I think about these things that charismatics believe other "thinking" people have ripped to shreds? Charismatics, perhaps more now than ever, need a fresh theological consciousness.

I believe that this book is a step forward into that Brave New World. Be patient with it. Don't read it to finish it. Read it to understand it. In doing so, maybe you'll play a part in implementing the Biblical foundation we need.

Nathan Finochio
Teaching Pastor, Hillsong NYC
Founder, TheosUniversity

INTRODUCTION

One of the greatest sources of encouragement to me is the renewed hunger today for the Word of God, especially among young believers. In a culture saturated with superficiality and addicted to the often mindless interactions of social media, Christian leaders have too often resorted to reducing the Biblical content of their messages to a level resulting in spiritual starvation among the sheep. They have forgotten that the only authority the preacher carries is that of the message we have been given. If you dilute the message in the deluded idea it will make it more appealing, you dilute your authority. And in the end, people stop listening. And leave. And then we wonder why we are losing the younger demographic in church.

The Bible is meant to be a lethal weapon in our hands. But if we don't understand how to use it, it won't work for us. Or worse yet, it may backfire. That is what I see happening far too often.

This short book addresses ten things in the Bible we often get wrong, but need to get right. I hope it helps you.

As always, I want to acknowledge the wisdom and support given to me over nearly forty years by my wife Elaine. She never fails to sharpen my focus in every area of life. If you have heard me teach, you have heard her voice as clearly as you have heard mine.

I am grateful for the generous support of our friends Jason and Erika Tetzloff of Centreville, Michigan, which enabled the publication of this book, and for the design and editorial skills of my friend Joshua Best, creative director at davidandbrook.com, for its production.

And in all things, glory to God alone. Soli Deo Gloria.

Stratford, Ontario
June 2020

FAITH

People have many misconceptions of what true Biblical faith is. Here are some examples, all very current in the Christian world, followed by the Biblical antidotes.

First misconception: Believe as hard as you can. Some people think that faith is equivalent to the power of positive thinking, clad with a Christian veneer. It's like Spirit-led mind over matter. Once you've thought positively hard enough about all the things you want in life to the point you become totally convinced they will happen, then you speak them out as if already accomplished, and the results are guaranteed.

This kind of faith generally starts with the idea that God

wants you to be materially prosperous (see the chapter on money). Or that God wants you to be healthy. Or to have a happy family life. Or to become an influencer with a massive social media following. Or, more generally, that everything you want in life will come to pass and God will prevent any harm reaching your doorstep. Psalm 91 is often quoted to that end, which makes it interesting that the devil also quoted it to Jesus.

Your job then is to meditate on all these good things and become convinced in your mind that God will give them to you. Your posture of faith is what releases the harvest. Believe and you will receive.

But whatever you do, don't commit the fatal mistake, which is negative thinking or confession. Negative confession is refusing to think or speak any negative thought about myself. Refusing to entertain the possibility that God might be addressing sin or disobedience in my life. Refusing to believe that there might be something wrong about my pursuit of self-fulfillment. Therefore I am not going to speak words or think thoughts which allow for the possibility that what I want in life and what I've asked God to do for me may not happen. That can spoil your party really quickly. God will be displeased because above all he wants you to be you and get whatever you want. And God will not release blessing to you, because the release of blessing is determined in the end result by the words you speak. God is only a facilitator.

It's easy to see how with this kind of thinking God can become an accessory to your personal desires, in which case we are only one step away from remaking him in our own image and worshipping an idol.

The answer: Faith is not about believing as hard as you can. This brand of teaching originated over one hundred years ago in the writings of E.W. Kenyon. It has been argued that Kenyon was influenced by the teachings of Mary Baker Eddy, the founder of Christian Science. Eddy taught that true reality is spiritual, not physical. God did not create a material world. God is Mind, and Jesus is not God, only an example of someone who moved past the material world into spiritual reality. Healing can be obtained through rising to a spiritual plane and denying the reality of things happening at the physical level. Illness, in the last result, is not actually real. *It's an illusion which can be dispelled by correct belief.* Tragically, many Christian Scientists chose faith over medical treatment and wound up dead. Kenyon, for his part, rejected most of Eddy's teachings, but hit upon the thought that we could obtain physical healing through speaking a word of faith. He believed that all we needed to claim healing was to believe it in our mind and speak it with our lips.

Kenyon, in turn, had a massive impact on the theology of the Word of Faith movement. Many of its teachers are well known. I am not denying that God used these individuals. But I don't believe that healings came because they spoke words of faith without doubt and obligated God to produce what they wanted. I think they simply operated in Biblical gifts of healing or of faith sovereignly bestowed by God. Why otherwise would only some have been healed? Jesus was the only one to have a perfect success rate in the miraculous! I believe the faith teachers have confused a sovereignly-given gift of faith with the ordinary exercise of faith. Peter walked by the beggar at the temple's gates scores of times without ever feeling he had authority to pray for his healing — until that day when he received a gift of faith and spoke with great boldness to the man. We cannot presume to walk in a continuous exercise of a gift sovereignly given in God's own timing.

Things were further complicated by something Kenyon had not really envisioned: that the same words of faith which achieved divine healing could just as well be exercised to obtain other things. If there is no limit to what our mind can accomplish, and God is always at our disposal, why not go for broke? As time went on, the teaching percolated down to people who desperately wanted blessings from God in their own lives. That blessing may not have been physical healing at all. It might have been more to do with image, popularity, even physical appearance. Or the money needed to achieve those goals. I remember so clearly seeing a picture of a car on a fridge someone was claiming in faith whenever they opened the fridge door. Whatever the nuances of the teaching, what people *heard* was that all they needed to do was exercise the word of faith, and the material world would come into submission to their verbal confession. Needless to say, multitudes experienced little but disappointment.

Mary Baker Eddy's movement has largely disappeared, but vestiges of her influence have lived on. How many preachers out there are saying that by having the right attitude you can do anything you want, be anyone you want to be, and God's role is just to make you happy and self-fulfilled?

The truth is that our words cannot create anything. Faith is a gift from God. It is not something our mind creates through positive believing. This should be a relief for most of us. One of the most honest cries in the Bible came from the desperate father who cried out to Jesus, "I believe; help my unbelief!" (Mk. 9:23) It was that cry that moved Jesus to compassion and resulted in his prayer being answered. Faith is not a matter of how hard we believe. Faith occurs when God meets our desperation through his deliverance. Faith is not generated by the mind. It is birthed through the Holy Spirit planting in our spirit an assurance that

God is in charge even though we can scarcely believe it. The greatest prerequisite for receiving faith is an honest recognition that we cannot create it through mental belief or positive confession. The truth is that God's power is always revealed in our weakness, in our desperate cry for help. But think for a moment. If we could create faith through positive confession, and if the performance of miracles depends on our positive confession, then why do we need God other than as an accessory to our faith?

The faith movement has misinterpreted two Biblical texts in particular. The first is 2 Cor. 4:13: "I believed, and so I spoke." This is understood to mean that if we follow the two-step process of believing something we want and then speaking it out, God is obliged to meet our request. Apart from the fact God will not be controlled that way, this is not what Paul means. The apostle is in the midst of a painful crisis with the Corinthian church, one that has left him in despair and depression. And so he quotes Psalm 116:10: "I believed, even when I spoke, 'I am greatly afflicted; I said in my alarm, 'All mankind are liars.'" His faith in God leads him to the honest confession of his doubts! Like the psalmist, he speaks out his disillusionment and frustration, but does so in order to bring that disappointment to God and ask for help and mercy. In the midst of his despair over the betrayal of the Corinthian believers for whom he has laid down his life, he cries out to God, giving his pledge of maintaining faith in God and loyalty to the gospel in spite of the disasters unfolding around him. To "believe" is not mental assent to certain prayer requests. *To believe is to remain faithful to God in spite of the circumstances.* His mind was telling him to give up, but deep in his spirit, and in the midst of his doubts, he cried out to God that he would remain faithful. God often shows up in the midst of our desperation. He meets us, as the theologian N.T. Wright put it, "at the screaming point." That is a hard place to be, but it's often the place we meet the Lord.

The second misinterpreted text is Mark 11:23-24: "Truly, I say to you, whoever says to this mountain, 'Be taken up and thrown into the sea,' and does not doubt in his heart, but believes that what he says will come to pass, it will be done for him. Therefore I tell you, whatever you ask in prayer, believe that you have received it and it will be yours." Looking at the Mount of Olives, which at that moment he was facing, he tells his disciples that *if they believe and do not doubt,* they can speak to *this mountain* and tell it to be cast into the sea. The reference to the mountain can only be understood in light of the passage Jesus is alluding to in Zechariah 14. There, the Mount of Olives (the same mountain Jesus is telling us to speak to) will be split in two, and a river will flow from the Mediterranean to the Dead Sea. Jesus is referring to the coming of the kingdom, initiated in his earthly ministry and culminating at his return. Mountains in the Old Testament represent strongholds, either of God or of the enemy. In this case, the Mount of Olives represents something standing in the way of the will of God. When the kingdom comes, it will break the mountain in two. Jesus is telling us is that we have authority to ask God to remove anything which stands against the eternal purposes of God. He does not say that we have authority to name and claim anything we want. *We can only ask God for what is in his eternal will.*

Despite the undoubted ways God has used many of its leaders, the Word of Faith movement has unintentionally diminished God by exalting our response to him as the critical factor in what he does. In the end, we wind up with a smaller concept of God, and a bigger concept of what in the end is our own useless humanity. We live in a world which sets out to make us little gods, which says that image and appearance are everything, but sooner or later we find out it doesn't work. And that's when we need to find a real God, a God who is not at our beck and call, a God who is sovereign but who comes into our world of failure and sets us free.

It should be a massive relief to us that God looks at our heart obedience, not the day to day state of our mind and thoughts. He understands the struggles we are going through trying to pay off student debt, maintain an image on social media, pay the mortgage, raise kids and work for employers who demand everything but don't give any security in return. That's a tough place to be. God wants to take us in our place of weakness and give us strength to get through it.

Second misconception: Faith is a feeling. Some folk measure their faith by their feelings. A person with real faith is on a spiritual high all of the time. By contrast, the presence of doubt, depression and despair mean I have no faith at all. People like this often equate spiritual maturity with being on a constant emotional high. And then begin to doubt their salvation when they have bad days.

If we live in our feelings, then our feelings tell us who we really are. How can I be a strong Christian if I wake up feeling depressed or with anxiety? Surely the Bible says we are more than conquerors?

People like this often enter into a condition which could be described as being spiritually bi-polar. On bad days they are really down. We assume God is displeased with us on that account. What failures we are! On the other hand, on good days, when they get a spiritual high, they think they are the only people with true faith. They are God's answer to every church. They live closer to the Lord than their pastor does, and they make sure to let him know. But by the time the pastor comes looking for them to do something productive, they're down again and too defeated to help out.

The answer: Faith is not about what you feel. If faith is not produced by the mind, neither is it manufactured by the emotions. Abraham, whose ups and downs of emotion are recorded for us in detail, was a great example of faith. Paul was certainly another. Yet most of his second letter to the Corinthians is dominated by descriptions of the extreme highs and lows of his emotions as he dealt with an ungrateful and rebellious church.

Things came to such a state that Paul said it felt like a "sentence of death" had been passed on him. He was burdened far beyond his strength and despaired of life itself. He goes on to speak of affliction and anguish of heart, of many tears, of having no internal peace while he awaits the outcome of his appeal to the congregation through Titus, the representative he has sent. He paints a powerful picture through four figures of speech: afflicted but not crushed; perplexed but not driven to despair, persecuted but not forsaken; struck down, but not destroyed. The last phrase was translated in one version of the Bible this way: "knocked down, but not knocked out."

The Psalms are full of the honest and anguished cries of people whose emotions are all over the place. Think of the phrase, used so often, "How long, O Lord, how long?"

We judge our faith wrongly if we see its health as measured by the current state of our emotions. If faith is not a matter of the mind, neither is it a matter of the emotions.

Faith arises in our spirit when the Spirit of God breathes life into us. I don't imagine the blind beggar was having a great day emotionally. Life was a living nightmare for him. But then he heard Jesus was coming along the road. Something arose within his spirit that enabled him, against all that was ranged against him internally, to cry out for help. And Jesus answered him with these extraordinary words: "Your faith has made you well" (Mk. 10:52).

I am not saying that the emotions or the mind are unimportant to God. God desires to restore our minds and heal our emotions. But neither of them are the place where faith is born or where faith is exercised. Faith operates at a much deeper level.

I have had unexpected encounters with God at times of great emotional despair. God simply came in and helped me. Not because of anything I felt, or anything I thought in my mind. Both were places of hopelessness. But that is where the greatness and the sovereign power of God is at work, and where as a result God is most glorified.

Toward the end of 2 Corinthians, Paul sums up the deepest truth God has taught him in the pain of Christian leadership. His power is made perfect in only one place — our weakness.

And that is where I find hope. No matter what I feel like, it does not take away from the fact that God is able and

God is merciful. His plan for my life will not be ruined because I'm having a down day.

Feelings are not the true measurement of faith. To live in our feelings is to live in the ultimate echo chamber and to become more and more detached from reality. Faith is found in my heartfelt commitment to live according to the word of God. Faith is to be faithful is obedience to him. His only prerequisite is that I remain faithful. Having done all, like a bloodied boxer after fifteen rounds, I am still standing. If my only qualification is that I haven't walked out, that is the only qualification I am likely to need to receive God's help.

Third misconception: Faith is a doctrine. This category is a little harder to describe. These people usually reside in conservative churches with a heavy emphasis of teaching Biblical truth. And of course there's nothing wrong with that. They see faith as the content of Biblical doctrine. Faith consists of a large number of things we believe about God. Everything from creation to the Exodus to the law and on to the cross.

Mature Christian faith, in their view, is measured by endless study of truth. Church services are focussed on lengthy lectures bookended by a couple of hymns or, more daringly, contemporary worship songs, but these are added extras, not the heart. The best leaders are the best educated leaders. The Christians with the best faith are those who know the most about the Bible.

The answer: Faith is not about believing a list of doctrines. As a pastor, I never felt happy about making assent to a list of doctrinal statements a condition of fellowship. I had seen too many people agree to such statements, yet with precious little fruit of the Spirit in their lives.

Believing things about God — even correct things — does not make you a Christian. Of course, it is difficult to claim you are a Christian unless you do believe the record of the Bible. But such belief is not what gives you faith.

Faith is the heart cry of a man or woman when, realizing they cannot help themselves, they find a Saviour who can. That is the foundation of Christian faith. I agreed to a long list of things when I received confirmation in my home church as a teenager, but they did not become real to me until several years later when I had a personal encounter with Christ.

Please don't get me wrong. I have spent my life teaching the Word. I speak in many churches, write books and blogs, and teach in Christian colleges and seminaries. Truth is an utterly vital issue to me. But no one's faith is built on assent to doctrine. That is the building. The foundation is Christ himself. I once attended a seminary renowned for its educational standards and reverence for Scripture, and the year I spent there was a great blessing. But the longer I hung around it, the more I felt the pursuit of knowledge was overtaking the pursuit of God in my life. Was it me? Was it something in the environment? Or was it both?

All I know is that knowledge can be a dangerous thing. It was the fruit of that tree that the enemy encouraged our ancestors to take, and that was their downfall. If our faith and our churches are not firmly and daily rooted in a living personal experience of Christ through the Spirit, the same enemy will come after us. And knowledge will become an end in itself. That alone, in my opinion, explains so many cases where supposedly faithful Christians, even entire denominations over time, abandon the truth of the Bible. Mere possession of correct doctrine will not keep you against the wiles of the enemy. Only Christ will. And if you truly pursue Christ, he will look after your doctrine. If you are rooted and grounded in a local church where the word of God is consistently preached and lived out and where you are encouraged to seek a real and deep relationship with Christ, you won't have to worry too much about getting your doctrine right. It'll be just fine.

Fourth misconception: Faith is authenticity. This is the opposite of the previous category. These people disdain the study of doctrine and prefer to focus on a lifestyle which is, in their words, authentic. What is authentic, of course, is never really described. Other than it is to be "true to me." To have authentic faith is to be yourself, to be able to move seamlessly from church to world without missing a beat. To be authentic is to be able to define your own identity, to have your own truth. What the Bible may have to say about that becomes secondary or advisory.

My identity, on this view, is expressed outwardly in the image I try to project. Faith becomes about image. And image ultimately is about what other people think of me. Pretty soon I allow my faith to be determined by whether or not the pagan culture I live in likes it. Real faith becomes all about understanding that culture and relating positively to it. In fact, being accepted by it. Real faith is never judgmental. It loves people. Love wins, after all. Isn't that what Jesus practiced?

The authenticity people, the opposite of the doctrine crowd, are folk who tend to define faith in private and personal terms, and who increasingly resist commitment to local churches. They love God, but don't want anyone asking too many questions about what's going on in their lives. Faith takes on a cultural dimension. It's one part of who I am, but not the only part. Faith competes with work, pursuit of material things, leisure and so on. Faith for these people is an add-on to the rest of their lives. Many were raised in church, but have partly or fully walked away. Their identity is becoming more and more rooted in the pagan culture around them, but they don't even realize it. Or if they do, they may not be bothered by it. Yet in their own minds, they still believe, and the person who calls them out on the depth of their commitment will not receive a big hug.

The answer: Faith is obedience, not authenticity. At the beginning and end of Romans, Paul uses a phrase, the "obedience of faith." It stands like bookends to the body of important truth in between.   In Greek, the phrase carries this meaning: obedience is faith, and faith is obedience. Our Christian life begins with an expression of obedience to receive Christ as Lord, and that obedience is the hallmark of any real Christian experience.

Any true definition of faith must include obedience at its heart. And obedience is spelled out for us many ways in the Bible. Obedience includes faithful commitment to the body of Christ. Obedience includes walking in accountability. Obedience includes placing what God wants above job, career, money, friends or anything else.

People of faith place Christ at the centre, not the periphery. Faith is costly and demands sacrifice. This is not legalism; it is the expression of a heart sold out to God which knows it owes him a debt we can never repay.

I don't like the word authentic, at least in its current usage, because I think it's little more than an excuse for justifying the way I want to live and giving myself a pat on the back for doing it. If faith were truly authentic, it would not look like it does in the lives of many who claim to make authenticity their calling card. Faith is defined by a man who hung on a Roman cross, not someone who is an influencer with a big social media following. Yet that man had more influence on the history of the world while he was hanging there helplessly than anyone else before or since.

Fifth misconception: Faith is open-ended. This is a more highly-developed version of the previous option. Real faith is inclusive. It is open to what others have to say. It's about dialogue and acceptance, not about imposing our views on others. None of us can claim we have a monopoly on truth, so faith morphs into something like the ability to believe generalities about God while accepting the generalities other people believe about God, even if they don't believe the same generalities we do. We all have our own truth. We all speak our own truth. I have my faith and you have yours, but the key is we are open to each other. Faith exists alongside doubt. In fact, doubt is an essential part of faith. To claim otherwise is narrow and judgmental. Even when we're less and less sure who Jesus really is, one thing we do know is he loved everybody.

The answer: Faith is exclusive, not open-ended. The Gospel is described by Paul as a *skandalon*, an offence to the world. It's particularly an offence to the postmodern world in which we live, where truth is remade in the image of whoever is defining it. A world where everyone has their own truth is built on a lie. For what happens when my truth collides with your truth? That's where open-endedness and inclusivity grinds to a jarring and hypocritical halt. Many of the most professedly inclusive sectors of our culture are in fact extremely narrow-minded and even bigoted when it comes to people who dare to take issue with them. I can be inclusive and you can be inclusive — until what you believe about yourself affects my world of belief and begins to limit me. And so we have culture wars between feminists and transgendered, both of whom profess to believe in ultimate inclusivity. In the end, whoever has more power will impose their views on others. In a world without an eternal standard of truth, might always becomes right. Think of Russia in 1917, of Germany in 1933, of China in 1949.

The problem goes right back to the Garden, where we tried to take hold of the knowledge of good and evil. Ever since then, humanity has been attempting to establish its own understanding of good and evil, of what is true and what is not, in rebellion against God, who alone has the right to determine it.

The world is fine, as C.S. Lewis pointed out, with the idea of Jesus as a great moral teacher, but less so with the man who declared he was *the* truth, *the* way and *the* life. Yahweh revealed himself to Israel, but made clear he had given the other nations of the world over to the worship of pagan gods. Yahweh made no apology for this act of favoritism. But in return, he demanded that Israel worship him and him alone. And to the degree that Israel turned away from him, he handed them over to earthly judgments, sometimes horrendous. Jesus likewise reveals himself as the exclusive and only way to salvation, and the early church declared the same message. There is salvation is no other name.

So faith can never be open-ended. Yahweh is not interested in co-habiting with other gods. He demands our exclusive allegiance. And Jesus does the same. People who have reached this stage in their pilgrimage have passed outside the pale of Biblical Christianity. Whether they realize it or not, they are already dabbling in the worship of other gods. They think they have faith and are incensed when others suggest they don't, but God has already finished with them. At least, unless and until they repent.

I never cease to be amazed at how ignorant people are of church history. Why is this an issue? Because we have believed the lie that the moment we ourselves are living in right now is the only moment that matters. If that is the case, we are truly doomed to repeat all the mistakes past generations made, because we have refused to learn about them or learn from them. We are not living at the apex of human progress. We live in a fractured and broken society where one generation has run up so much debt it has wrecked the financial future of the generations following. To live in the moment is to put yourself in a prison.

The history of the Bible shows us that when people engage in idolatry, destruction is not far behind. The history of churches who have committed to "inclusivity" and walked away from God's truth tells a tale. Every denomination that has walked away from true faith and from exclusive allegiance to Jesus Christ has sooner or later disappeared. The evidence of that is all around us. Most liberal Protestant denominations, which held dominance as recently as my younger years, are projected to disappear entirely over the next decade or two. Their lampstand has been removed, even while they still talk loudly about being people of faith.

Faith is not accommodation to the values of the secular culture around us, and then despising those who refuse to follow that lead. *Christianity at its most genuine and healthy is a counter-cultural movement.* The culture we live in is sick and dying. It is not a culture we want to accommodate, but to challenge. But to do it, we need to have our faith anchored in something bigger than an echo chamber in which we speak our own truth to no one but ourselves.

LAST WORDS ABOUT FAITH

Faith is a gift from God, given in response to our receiving Christ as Lord of our lives. Faith is rooted in the encounter between the Holy Spirit and our spirit, what Paul describes as the "inner person." It is not anchored in our mind or emotions, but in God himself. The Greek word "to believe" is *pisteuo*, and its fundamental meaning is to place our trust in a person. Once we have done that, God helps us ground our mind and our emotions in himself. Over the long term the reality of faith, as Jesus pointed out, is measured by the fruit of obedience to God in our lives. And that's not legalism. It's simply taking the temperature of where our life is at with the Lord. By our fruits, as Jesus said, we will be known. God will nourish our faith by the presence of the Spirit. We need the continuous re-filling of the Spirit for our faith to stay healthy. The Holy Spirit will show us what to pray and believe for, and it will always be in alignment with the Word of God and the will of God. Faith is ultimately faithfulness. Those with great faith are those who, when all is said and done, remain faithful. And those who remain faithful God will never disappoint. So take heart, you probably have more faith than you think!

WORSHIP

As a young believer, I was part of a revolution in worship. The music changed and so did the instruments. We went from old hymns accompanied by piano and organ to new choruses accompanied by guitar and drums.

It was messy. A lot of older people found themselves caught in a musical tsunami. But what drove the revolution was not just changing taste in music or instruments. It was a spontaneous movement toward expressing what was happening in the hearts of millions of young people in the musical forms and instrumentation they were at home with.

The revolution rolled on, and eventually transformed the dynamics of public worship in almost every kind of church.

But along the way, something else happened. Worship music, which had started with anonymous people writing songs for their own churches, went corporate. And what had begun as a move of the Spirit wound up as an industry. Now we had artists and performers trying to break into the big time.

And what was happening in the big picture was only a reflection of what was going on in local churches. Worship was becoming a performance.

It may be just me, but I haven't encountered a lot of Biblically-based teaching on worship. Worship seminars are mostly lessons in how to conduct worship, train teams, run the sound booth, develop a live-stream, help people in song-writing and so on. All those things are necessary, particularly in the technically-complicated world of sound and light in which we live. But, taken on their own, they are a building without a foundation.

What happened in the Jesus movement was profound and game-changing for one reason: it was birthed out of a powerful visitation of God in which millions of young people were swept into the kingdom. And where the Holy Spirit was present, the worship turned out right, even without the seminars. People were genuine participants, and not just members of an audience.

God can do amazing things through the sheer moving of the Holy Spirit, but he expects us in due course to build a Biblical foundation under what we are experiencing, or else in time we will lose it. We will have the outward form, but without the substance.

Perhaps I am being too harsh. And I'm not suggesting every worship leader has a secret desire to be a Nashville star. But increasingly, worship leaders I speak to are sharing the same concerns I have, and are looking for help.

That's what I'm going to try to provide here.

THE FOUNDATION OF ALL WORSHIP

The chief goal of humanity is to glorify God and to enjoy him. So says the Westminster Confession, one of the great Christian statements of faith, written four hundred years ago but still carrying magnificent truth for today. One of the chief ways we glorify God is to worship him. If that is the case, worship must become a much greater priority in our lives, and we must understand more about it than we have done in the past. One of the sad things about worship is the way believers argue over forms of worship without really understanding what worship is. If we understood worship more deeply, we would argue about its outward forms much less.

WHAT IS WORSHIP?

A good place to start is in Romans 12:1. In the first eleven chapters of Romans, Paul has laid out the entirety of the Gospel, all that God has done for us in Christ. Romans 12:1 is a kind of hinge on which the whole letter turns from a description of what God has done to a consideration of what we must do in return. And the very first and most critical thing is worship. Worship is presented as the offering up of our lives to God: "Present yourselves a sacrifice, living, holy and pleasing to God, which is your reasonable [properly understood] service of worship" (Rom. 12:1, my translation). When we present ourselves to God, we present our lives in their entirety. This sacrifice causes us to pass out of our own ownership and into God's. If we have not understood that, we have not made the sacrifice. We can talk of giving up many things, but the only thing that really matters is the giving up of our independence. If you haven't given up your independence, you haven't really given up anything.

This sacrifice is to be *living*, an expression of our new life in Christ offered back to him. It is to be *holy*, signifying that our new life does not belong to us and that we do not have the right to live it as we want. And it is to be *pleasing to God*. God will never accept defective sacrifices. A true sacrifice, one in which nothing is withheld and the best of what we are is presented to God, will always be accepted. To present our lives to God in this way "is your reasonable worship." Or to put it the way I suggested above, it is "worship, properly understood."

The laying down of our lives is worship as God truly understands it. If the outward expression of worship is the honoring of God with our lips, our voices and our bodies, then the foundation of worship is the honoring of God in the complete submission and sacrifice of our lives and our hearts to him. When we have reached the point of being willing to serve Christ no matter what the cost, we have come to the true meaning of worship.

Whatever else worship is when we come together to praise the Lord, it amounts to nothing more than religious ritual (whether Catholic, Baptist or charismatic) unless it is accompanied by the laying down of our lives. The laying down of our lives constitutes the essential foundation for the rest of our worship. We can come before God with all sorts of songs, prayers and other acts, but unless it involves more than that, our worship is meaningless. The "heart of worship," to use Matt Redman's phrase, is the willingness to offer up our lives as a sacrifice to God.

Worship begins with God. Worship, like faith, is a gift from God. We can only believe in God and enter into relationship with him because he gives us the ability to do so. Worship takes us into the very presence of God and transforms us. What a tragedy if this gift of worship were set aside, wasted or lost!

Worship is a form of communication. It is the expression, in word and deed, of our praise and thanksgiving to God for who he is and what he has done for us. God would deserve our worship even if he had not sent his Son to die for us, simply because he is our Creator. But how much more should we worship him because of the great love and mercy he has shown us! Worship is a transaction between our spirit and God, made possible by the presence of God the Holy Spirit dwelling within us. If worship is a transaction between our spirit and God, in which the Holy Spirit enables us to offer our praise to God, then worship must grow out of our fellowship or relationship with God.

Yet worship is still a choice. If we allow worship to be dictated by our emotions or our circumstances, it will quickly wither away into an occasional gust of thanks during moments where we are feeling good. True worship, however, is modeled by Job. After losing his sons and daughters and all his possessions, he fell on his face and cried out: "The Lord gives and the Lord takes away. Blessed be the name of the Lord" (Job 1:21).

Throughout the Bible, worship is connected with the presence of God. Our response to God's presence is worship. Worship can be personal or corporate. Music is an expression of worship. So also is prayer, whether in a corporate or individual setting. As we sing or as we pray, we acknowledge who God is and what he has done for us.

A BRIEF HISTORY OF WORSHIP

The temple of the Garden. The Garden was also a temple. We know that because the same words used in God's job description for Adam, to "work" and "keep" the Garden, are also used of the activities of the priests in the tabernacle. In the Garden, God's presence and communication was perfect. Every time they met him and responded to him, Adam and Eve were worshipping him. In the temple of the Garden, God's presence was freely accessible. When humanity fell, this perfect worship was lost. Yet God is gracious, and he continued to reveal himself to people. His purpose has always been to restore worship to what it had been in the Garden.

The beginnings of restoration. Worship cannot take place without God being present. And God's presence was never fully withdrawn from the earth. Not long after humanity had been cast out of the Garden, we find God allowing Cain and Abel to approach him in worship (Gen. 4:3-4). One generation later, people began to call on the name of the Lord (Gen. 4:26). Later, Noah built an altar to the Lord (Gen. 8:20). When God appeared first to Abraham, Abraham responded by building an altar so that he could worship God (Gen. 12:7). Then he built a second altar, the purpose of which was so to call on the name of the Lord (Gen. 12:8). God revealed himself to Jacob in a dream. When Jacob awoke, he built an altar and called the name of the place Bethel ("house of God" in Hebrew), because "this is none other than the house of God, and this is the gate of heaven" (Gen. 28:17).

The tabernacle of Moses. In the same way, God came to Moses many times, beginning with the encounter at the burning bush (Exod. 3:2). Moses is a prototype of restoration, a model of what God wants to do in restoring his presence and restoring worship to his people. Moses had a revelation of worship. The first words he spoke to Pharaoh were: "Thus says the Lord, the God of Israel, 'Let my people go, that they may hold a feast to me in the wilderness" (Exod. 5:1). Repeatedly, he demanded that Pharaoh allow the Israelites to worship God (Exod. 7:16; 8:1; 9:1, 13; 10:3). The deliverance of the children of Israel from Egypt was all about the restoration of worship. Moses knew how to worship the Lord. God himself spoke these words about him: "If there is a prophet among you, I the Lord, make myself known to him in a vision; I speak with him in a dream. Not so with my servant Moses. He is faithful in all my house. With him I speak mouth to mouth, clearly, and not in riddles, and he beholds the form of the Lord" (Num. 12:6-8).

Through Moses, the most significant step in the restoration of worship thus far in the Bible occurred. God allowed his presence to dwell in a particular place. From the moment the tabernacle was completed, it was attended constantly by the cloud and the pillar of fire, signifying the presence of God (Exod. 40:35-38). According to Heb. 5:6, the tabernacle was a model of what already existed in heaven. The tabernacle in heaven represents the ultimate restoration of worship. Moses' tabernacle, as a model of this heavenly reality, was a significant step in the process of restoration. The cherubim over the ark represented the angels placed at the entrance to the garden, guarding access to the presence of God. The Holy of Holies was like the Garden in miniature, which explains not only the cherubim but also the lampstand (representing the tree of life) as well as the pomegranates and gourds. Even the jewels on the High Priest's breastpiece represented the same jewels found in the Garden. The Holy of Holies contained the presence of God, it contained God's communication to humanity, and it contained the authority he had given us – all things Adam and Eve had enjoyed. Yet it was also guarded by the cherubim put in place to ensure that, until the curse was lifted, humanity would not have direct access to his presence.

The tabernacle of David.   After a long period of spiritual decline, in which at one point the ark was seized by the Philistines, David realized how precious the presence of God was.   His heart yearned for the restoration of what Israel had known under Moses.   He decided to bring the ark up from Kiriath-jearim to a place of honor in his new capital of Jerusalem.   After one failed attempt in which the instructions the Lord had given to Moses were not followed (2 Sam. 6:7), David succeeded.   The Levites carried the ark as Moses had ordered (1 Chron. 15:2-15).   There was tremendous celebration – shouting, dancing, singing and the playing of many instruments (1 Chron. 15:16-24). David himself worshipped with such energy and intensity that his unspiritual wife Michal despised him and came under God's judgment (1 Chron. 15:27-29, 2 Sam. 6:20-23). Finally, David placed the ark inside a tent he had pitched for it (1 Chron. 16:1).

David appointed Levites, in line with the command of the law, "as ministers before the ark of Lord, to invoke, to thank, and to praise the Lord, the God of Israel" (1 Chron. 16:4). He appointed Asaph the Levite and his family as worship leaders in the tabernacle, and to carry on this joyous form of worship continually with singing and instruments (1 Chron. 16:7, 37). He appointed the sons of Asaph, Jeduthun and Heman to prophesy, give thanks and sing before the Lord's presence in Jerusalem. Those involved in worship were numbered in multiples of twelve, twelve being the Biblical number of government. This reminds us that worship is more than just our expression of praise to God. It is an important part of the exercise of God's government and authority on earth, for through it his presence becomes manifest in our midst and his power begins to operate.

The intriguing thing about David's tabernacle is that people were apparently able to worship before the ark. There is no record of a Holy of Holies into which the high priest alone could enter. The tabernacle was at Gibeon (1 Chron. 16:39), where the sacrifices were offered until the time of Solomon.

The account says that the Levites (not the priests) ministered before the ark of the Lord (1 Chron. 16:4). But we know a lot more about what went on at the tabernacle of David, for many of the songs of worship were written by David, by Asaph or by Asaph's family members, and are recorded for us in the Book of Psalms. Although we no longer have the musical accompaniment, we have the substance of the words, and these are words which have been put to music again and again over the ages. It's as if God made a distinction between what is permanent and what is transitory or temporary. He caused the words to stand forever, but left the music to change from age to age, so that the power and meaning of the words could be applied in a relevant and meaningful way to every nation and culture. So the music is never to be put on a level with the words. And where do we argue most over worship? About the music! Why? Because we are trying to make what is transitory permanent, what is relative absolute. Our priority should be to make sure there is real Biblical substance in the words we are singing. If we got it right on that, there might be less discord and more harmony, both in the Spirit and in the music!

The decline of worship. David's tabernacle was replaced by a far grander structure, the temple of Solomon. God graced the temple with his supernatural presence while Solomon was alive (2 Chron. 5:14; 7:1-2). The temple was plundered by the Egyptians within five years of his death, and fell into long periods of disrepair as the spiritual life of the nation declined. Eventually, both the temple and the ark were destroyed by the Babylonians. After the exile, the temple as rebuilt under Zerubbabel (Ezra 1-3), but as a shadow of its former self. After the last of the prophets died out, the Jewish people believed the presence of God had departed from the nation. Shortly before the time of Jesus, Herod the Great destroyed the temple of Zerubbabel, and in its place built a temple which was more a monument to himself than to God, and it was this temple whose destruction Jesus announced (Mt. 24:2).

The temple of Jesus. Jesus told the people it had taken 46 years to build Herod's temple, but that he would raise it up in three days (Jn. 2:19). This new temple, spoken of by Jesus, would bring the restoration of worship to its earthly climax. Jesus did away with need for a physical temple when he rent the veil and opened the way into the Holy of Holies by his sacrifice on the cross. This is richly described for us in Hebrews chapter 9. When the Holy Spirit fell at Pentecost, he filled the believers and brought them into the temple of Jesus. This is a spiritual building whose cornerstone is Christ (Eph. 2:20-22). In it we are all priests who offer up sacrifices to God (1 Pet. 2:5). Instead of being defined as a people of a particular race or geographical nation congregating at a sacred building to witness a select group of priests offering sacrifices to God on our behalf, we are now peoples of every race and nation, all priests to God, gathering together throughout the world irrespective of where we meet. When Jesus spoke of the destruction of the temple and its replacement, he was talking not just about the nature of the church as opposed to Israel, but also about the restoration of worship and of the temple of the Garden. When he made the statement that the temple was his body, he pointed to the coming end of the physical temple, and with it the abolition of all restrictions on entry into the presence of God for any believer in Christ. For the first time since the Garden, men and women, no matter where they lived, could encounter God's presence. Even in the time of David, that was not so, for even though the ark was in open view, you had to go to where it was to experience God's presence.

The early church realized the significance of the tabernacle of David. What the tabernacle of David pointed toward was fulfilled in the temple of Jesus. When the apostles and elders met together in Jerusalem to debate how the Gospel was going to move forward into the Gentile world, Peter pointed to the prophecy of Amos 9:11-12 as the key: "After this I will return, and I will rebuild the tent of David that has fallen; I will rebuild its ruins, and I will restore it, that the remnant of mankind may seek the Lord, and all the Gentiles who are called by my name, says the Lord, who makes these things known from of old" (Ac. 15:16-18).

The church is to be characterized by the presence of God with his people, and this has massive implications for worship. The tabernacle of David was the high point of old covenant worship. It was the place where the presence of God was manifest to the people, not just the High Priest. And it was the place where old covenant worship went beyond offering sacrifices to the unrestrained offering of peoples' hearts in thanksgiving and praise to God. But this is only a foretaste of worship in the temple of Jesus.

THE RELEASE OF THE MANIFEST PRESENCE OF GOD

There are two critical characteristics of worship in the temple of Jesus. The first is the release of the manifest presence of God.

In one sense, God is everywhere: "Where shall I go from your Spirit? Or where shall I flee from your presence? If I ascend to heaven, you are there! If I make my bed in Sheol, you are there!" (Ps. 139:7-8). Yet we may not be aware of it. In the Garden, God was visibly and undeniably present. When we fell, we lost the reality of that presence, and with it most of our ability to worship. The Bible is a record of the plan of God to restore the manifest sense of his presence which was there in the Garden. This occurred dramatically, but in a limited and restricted way, when the glory of God came down on Moses' tabernacle and again on Solomon's temple. Both of these were miniature replicas of the Garden, with the cherubim signifying that the presence was still drastically restricted. But now we live in the temple of Jesus, that temple in which all of us can come into the Holy of Holies. *This temple represents the restoration of the Garden, to the extent it can be restored on earth.* Wherever the church gathers, there is the possibility of the manifest presence of God coming down, and along with it the release of his eternal and supernatural power. This was imprinted into the DNA of the church at its birth and runs like a thread throughout the book of Acts.

Since the destruction of the ark, the presence of the Spirit had disappeared from the earth. The Jews spoke of four hundred years of silence, during which there was no word from God. They looked forward to the day the Messiah would come. They believed that the sign of his coming would involve two things: fire and the return of the Spirit. That is why the thousands who gathered at Pentecost to witness the outpouring of the Spirit upon the first disciples were attracted not by preaching, *but by the manifestation of God's presence in the worship of the believers.* For the first time since the destruction of Solomon's temple over six hundred years before, the manifest presence of God had returned to the earth. And it was happening not as when the presence was restricted to a place only one man could go but, like the tabernacle of David, it was happening right out in the open amongst the people. As the manifest presence of God came down on the church, the church responded in supernaturally-empowered worship, and this presence and the worship which accompanied it proved to the people of Jerusalem that Jesus Christ was the Messiah. No wonder the worship opened the door for Peter to preach the Gospel, and no wonder three thousand people were saved!

When the church was threatened by the authorities, they gathered together to pray and worship God, and the power of God was released in such a manner that the building they were in was shaken by an earthquake, and they were all filled with the Holy Spirit (Ac. 4:31). The manifest presence of God was so powerful that signs and wonders were taking place as they gathered together for worship in the portico of the temple (Ac. 5:12). As Peter left the worship gathering, the presence of God was still so powerfully upon him that the sick were healed as his shadow fell on them (Ac. 5:15) – a miracle not even attributed to Jesus. The people of the city and surrounding areas were bringing the sick and the demonized into the worship gatherings, and there they were being healed (Ac. 5:16). The commissioning of the apostle Paul came during a time of worship in the church at Antioch (Ac. 13:1). A second earthquake precipitated by worship is recorded in Ac. 16:25-26. The worship in the Philippian jail had only two participants – Paul and Silas. They did not need to be in a crowd of thousands to receive the blessings of God and see the jail doors break open. Sometimes we feel we have to be in a large worship gathering to be uplifted, then when we go home we lose the sense of God's presence. Paul and Silas teach us that each of us can access the presence of God anywhere we are and even in difficult circumstances. The secret of passionate corporate worship is often based on the fact that many of the worshippers have brought into the large gathering the richness of their own time with God during the week just ended.

THE PRIESTHOOD OF ALL BELIEVERS

The second critical characteristic of worship in the temple of Jesus is the priesthood of all believers. What does this mean for us in practice?

1. No one else is a priest for us. We realize that we do not need anyone else to enter the presence of God for us. That is what distinguishes us from Roman Catholics, for instance, who still have priests offering sacrifices at altars in temples every Sunday. But while we remember that *no one else is needed* to enter the presence of God for us, we forget that *no one else can* enter the presence of God for us. If we do not offer the sacrifice of our praise to God, no one else can do it for us. What this means is that when we gather together for worship, God expects each person to come as their own priest into his presence. Paul applied this practically to the church in Corinth: "When you come together, each one has a hymn, a lesson, a revelation, a tongue, or an interpretation" (1 Cor. 14:26).

2. It's not about the people at the front. Paul teaches that the body is not just one part, but is composed of all its parts (1 Cor. 12:14-26). Each part has a function, and that is true in worship. If one part is missing, the whole body loses out. Paul gives another picture of our worship gatherings in Col. 3:16: "Let the word of Christ dwell in you richly, teaching and admonishing one another in all wisdom, singing psalms and hymns and spiritual songs, with thankfulness in your hearts to God." The emphasis is on the involvement of the many, not just the few. Somehow we have to find ways of enabling verbal participation of the congregation in worship through prayer, reading of Scripture or spiritual gifts exercised in line with the theology of the local congregation. If worship is something exclusively involving the band and worship leaders, then they have become priests on our behalf, and we might as well set up a Holy of Holies at the front and wall it off.

3. Worship is to bless God, not us. When we focus on the people at the front, worship becomes an entertainment, an activity done by those people in order to make the rest of us feel better. That is not worship. Worship has nothing to do with anyone making anyone else feel good, cheered up, inspired, uplifted or anything else. Worship is about each one of us coming before God to glorify him and give him praise. Why is it that we have it the wrong way around? Of course, if God is pleased with our worship, he will send his presence into our midst and we will be touched – but that is not why we do it.

4. The danger of the default setting. Just like computers, human beings have a default setting. If we do not progress in

God, we will fall back into our old nature. That is part of the battle we face. God gives us the power of his Spirit to help us, but we have to open the door first. The default setting in worship is called passivity. I will sit back and expect God to bless me without my exercising my priestly duty to give him praise and glorify him. Worship is an action. It is something we do, not a mist or cloud we enter into in the hope that God will drop spiritual rain upon us.

5. The power of a worshipping priesthood. When the high priest brought the sacrifice into the presence of God on the Day of Atonement, he was able, through his act of worship, to ensure the favor of God upon the whole nation for another year. There was incredible power in his worship, and in the blessing it released on the nation. What would happen if each of us took up our high priestly duties, entered into the presence of God together and began to offer our worship to him? How much blessing of God would be released not only on us but also on the world around us? I am convinced that this is why one of Satan's primary goals is to confuse and deceive the people of God about the nature and power of worship, and to do anything he can to prevent them from taking up our privilege and responsibility as priests to enter into the presence of God. That is why worship in traditional churches is often reduced to dreary and ritualistic singing of hymns which once had great power but are now lifeless in the hands of people with no vision. That is why even in Bible-based churches, worship is often reduced to a loud band conducting a performance at the front which the rest of the congregation observes in somewhat deafened passivity, not even able to hear the sound coming out of their own mouths as they sing. God wants something better. Jesus died so we could enter into his temple, and in that temple first access and then release the power of God.

The temple of the Lord God Almighty and the Lamb. No history of worship is complete without peering into the future for its final chapter. There is one further temple to be revealed: "And I saw no temple in the city, for its temple is the Lord God the Almighty and the Lamb" (Rev. 21:22). As the first book of the Bible reveals worship as it existed before the fall, so the last book illustrates worship after humanity's complete restoration. In this heavenly temple, we live and dwell continuously in the immediate and unrestricted presence of God, thus bringing the restoration of worship to its final fulfillment.

The Bible ends as it began, in a garden temple. The only difference is that in the last garden temple, the presence of evil has been cast out. John Piper has said that the ultimate goal of the church is not mission, but worship. Mission exists because and wherever worship does not. Where there is no worship, mission exists to bring people into the temple of God to worship him. The intention of God throughout human history has been to restore the worship we lost through our own sin, and to do so at his expense, ultimately through the blood of his Son. To fail to worship is not only to be careless, lazy or negligent, it is to sin, because it is our worship which not only gives God the honor he is due, but also releases the authority and power of God into the earth. The greatest exercise of your priesthood is to offer to God the sacrifice of your praise. It is not something that anyone else can do for you. Worship is our highest privilege. It is the ultimate expression of our relationship with God.

Of all the attacks of Satan on the church, none is more insidious or dangerous than his desperate attempts to keep God's people from worship. He will do it by distorting what it is, by diluting what it is, by minimizing what it is, by making it into nothing more than a religious exercise, and then by causing people to spend more time arguing about it than doing it. These are the days when God is calling his people to rise up, frustrate every attack of the evil one, and bring the worship of God back into his temple. And then we will see his kingdom come.

HEALING

From beginning to end, the Bible teaches that supernatural healing is a legitimate part of God's activity. He made us - why can he not heal us? Especially when one of his names is *Yahweh-rapha*, the Lord our healer (Exod. 15:26). This does not exclude proper consultation with doctors, nor does it overlook our responsibility to treat our bodies as temples of the Holy Spirit and keep healthy in the process. Nevertheless, there are times when we must and should call out to the Lord for help no doctor can give.

Healing is a significant part of our inheritance as Christians. It has often been misunderstood. It has been discarded where the church has lost touch with the desire of God to heal. It has been abused by unscrupulous individuals preying upon the sick for financial or ministry gain. It is hard to uphold in our western society where we have an abundance of medical help and where our belief system has become heavily influenced by the humanistic rationalism of our age. Yet healing is important to God. The Biblical concept of *shalom* involves wholeness of body, soul and spirit. It was very important to Jesus, who spent a good deal of his time engaged in it. It is vital for us to establish a Biblical understanding of healing upon which we can with confidence begin to move out in faith. In his outstanding book, *Power Healing* (Harper and Row, 1987, pages 170-172), John Wimber sketched out six basic principles. I use these principles here, fleshing them out with my own content, to provide us with a framework to understand Biblical healing.

FIRST PRINCIPLE: GOD WANTS TO HEAL THE SICK

When Jesus first sent his disciples out, he gave them this commission: "And he called to him his twelve disciples and gave them authority over unclean spirits, to cast them out, and to heal every disease and every affliction" (Mt. 10:1). To heal the sick was the very first thing Jesus called his disciples to do. In the story of the healing of the paralytic (Mt. 9:1-8), he demonstrated that forgiveness of sins and healing of the sick go hand in hand. Both are normal activities of the kingdom. Sickness entered the world through Adam's sin. It was never in the original intention of God. We are redeemed from the eternal penalty of the curse, yet still suffer the temporary effects of it in this imperfect world. The fact that there is sickness and that one day our mortal bodies will perish does not change the fact that at the cross God began to undo the work of the devil in all its dimensions, including this one.

Scripture indicates that God heals for four primary reasons:

God heals because it is in his nature to heal. He revealed himself to Israel in these words: "I am the Lord, your healer" (Exod. 15:26). To heal is part of the very character of God. He healed Abimelech and his family (Gen.20:17-18). He opened Sarah's womb (Gen. 21:1-2), and did the same for Leah (Gen. 29:31). He healed Miriam of her leprosy (Num. 12:10-15). He healed the pagan general Naaman, who came to Elisha for help his own gods could not offer (2 Kgs. 5:1-19).

In the same way, it was in the very nature of Jesus to heal: "And he went throughout all Galilee... proclaiming the gospel of the kingdom and healing every disease and every affliction among the people" (Mt. 4:23). "And wherever he came, in villages, cities or countryside, they laid the sick in the marketplaces and implored him that they might touch even the fringe of his garment. And as many as touched it were made well (Mk. 6:56). "And all the crowd sought to touch him, for power came out from him and healed them all" (Lk. 6:19).

It is no surprise that what Jesus did, he also commissioned his followers to do: "And they departed and went though the villages, preaching the gospel and healing everywhere" (Lk. 9:6). "Now many signs and wonders were regularly done among the people by the hands of the apostles... so that they even carried out the sick into the streets and laid them on cots and mats, that as Peter came by at least his shadow might fall on some of them. The people also gathered... bringing the sick and those afflicted with unclean spirits, and they were all healed" (Ac. 5:12-16).

God heals because he is compassionate. In his self-revelation to Moses, the very first thing God declares about himself is his compassion: "The Lord, the Lord, a God merciful and gracious" (Exod. 34:6). Jesus healed for the same reason: "He had compassion on them and healed their sick" (Mt. 14:14); "Jesus went throughout all the cities and villages... healing every disease and every affliction. When he saw the crowds, he had compassion for them..." (Mt. 9:35-36).

God heals because the demonstration of supernatural power gives authority to the preaching of the kingdom. When Jesus was challenged in his authority to forgive sin, he replied: "But that you may know that the Son of Man has authority on earth to forgive sins..." (Mt. 9:6). The healing was the proof of his authority to forgive. The passage concludes: "When the crowds saw it, they were afraid, and they glorified God, who had given such authority to men" (Mt. 9:8). Jesus said the same thing to the unbelieving crowd: "If I am not doing the works of my Father, then do not believe me; but if I do them, even though you do not believe me, believe the works, that you may know and understand that the Father is in me and I am in the Father (Jn. 10:37-38). When Peter and John were called to account before the Sanhedrin, their demonstration of authority left the religious leaders powerless to refute the Gospel message: "But seeing the man who was healed standing beside them, they had nothing to say in opposition" (Ac. 4:14). God does not need anything to authenticate his message, but in his mercy he has provided for the demonstration of supernatural power, often through healing, to be a means by which people who otherwise would not believe might come to faith.

God heals to bring glory to his name. When news came to Jesus that Lazarus was sick, Jesus replied: "This illness does not lead to death. It is for the glory of God, so that the Son of God may be glorified through it" (Jn. 11:4). When he was about to call Lazarus from the tomb, Jesus cried out: "Did I not tell you that if you believed you would see the glory of God?" (Jn. 11:40).

SECOND PRINCIPLE: THE IMPORTANCE OF CORPORATE MINISTRY

Gifts are given to many. According to 1 Cor. 12:12-31, within the body of Christ there is a widespread bestowal of spiritual gifts upon all the members. Of all these gifts, healing is the only one mentioned in the plural. The implication is that God desires to bestow many gifts of healing upon a significant number of believers. Scripture also teaches that it is the responsibility of the elders in every local body to anoint with oil and pray for healing (Jas. 5:14). James then enlarges the sphere of healing by urging all church members to confess their sins one to another and pray for each other that they may be healed (Jas. 5:16). Jesus sent all his disciples out with the commission to heal the sick (Lk. 9:1-6; 10:1-23).

Gifts are given for the body. In his teaching on the gifts of the Spirit Paul states: "To each is given the manifestation of the Spirit for the common good" (1 Cor. 12:7). In other words, though the gifts are given through individuals, they are not given to individuals, but rather to the body. Healing, like the other gifts, is not a possession of any particular member of the body but is rather a gift which passes through their hands on its way to the intended recipient.

The body extends outward. Healing was one of the main ways in which Jesus touched people and extended his spiritual family. Following his example, the early church lost no time

58

in bringing healing to the community (Ac. 3:1-10). The sick and demon-possessed were brought out into the streets to be healed (Ac. 5:15-16). Very few people will decline prayer for healing, if it is offered in a respectful way. Healing is a significant way in which we can take the joy of family and see others included in it.

THIRD PRINCIPLE: OUR FAITH IN GOD IS DEMONSTRATED BY ACTION

To believe in healing is not enough. We must move from an intellectual acceptance of healing into a Spirit-empowered practice of it. To make this transition involves understanding of three foundational truths:

Choosing to believe the Word moves us from hope to faith. Realizing that it is God's desire to heal and that the practice of healing is an activity of all God's people gives us great hope. But putting what we believe the Bible teaches into practice requires us to move from hope to faith: "Now faith is the assurance of things hoped for, the conviction of things not seen" (Heb. 11:1). When it comes to healing, it is not enough to hope that one day God will heal someone, and then sit back and watch. God is calling us to exercise faith. That means to step out in acts of obedience which are based on the assumption that what God says in his Word is true, even when circumstances tell us the opposite. This does not mean being presumptuous or foolish, but if we are the only one available to pray for someone who is sick and if they want to be prayed for, then we have a mandate from God to do so. And even if the person is not healed, they will be grateful for the care you showed them.

Genuine faith always produces action. We cannot separate believing and obeying. Paul uses the phrase "the obedience of faith" at the beginning and end of Romans. The meaning of the phrase is that obedience is faith and faith is obedience. The same point is made by James: "So also faith by itself, if it does not have works, is dead" (Jas. 2:17). Faith is not just an intellectual or religious exercise divorced from any practical application. The Hebrew word for faith, *emmuneh*, means both *faith* and *faithfulness*. You cannot have faith without being faithful. Faith must be walked out to be real and complete. Faith refuses to walk away when it sees someone in need of healing. Faith springs into action in the practical expression of praying for the sick person to be healed. Faced with a person discouraged after praying for someone and not seeing them healed, John Wimber reportedly told him to go back and pray for a thousand people for healing before returning to him with a further complaint, because that is how many people he himself prayed for before seeing one healed.

Obedience is not legalism. Obedience comes out of obeying the prompting of the Holy Spirit. Legalism comes out of a sense of religious obligation, forced upon us by people or by human traditions. In the New Testament, words for "obey" and words for "believe" both occur over 250 times. One complements the other. When we understand what the Bible says about God's desire to heal, how can we not respond?

FOURTH PRINCIPLE: THE EMPOWERING OF THE HOLY SPIRIT TO BE WITNESSES

Jesus himself relied on the Holy Spirit to do the works he did. Jesus told the disciples they would be clothed with power from on high (Lk. 24:49) and baptized with the Spirit (Ac. 1:5). The results were evident on the day of Pentecost. The disciples moved from fear into a faith that manifested itself in a constant flow of signs and wonders accompanying the rapid spread of the gospel. God's plan has not changed and his gifts have not ceased (see the chapter of prophecy). According to the Greek continuous present tense in Eph. 5:18, we need to be continually re-filled with the Spirit for the task of mission, including the ministry of healing.

The mandate given to believers is to be Christ's witnesses to the ends of the earth (Ac. 1:8). This has several applications in relation to healing:

We are witnesses to the Biblical fact of healing. Peter brought the Gospel to the Gentiles in these words: "You yourselves know what happened... how God anointed Jesus of Nazareth with the Holy Spirit and with power. He went about doing good and healing all who were oppressed by the devil... And we are witnesses of all that he did both in the country of the Jews and in Jerusalem" (Ac. 10:37-39). Even if we have never witnessed an actual miracle of healing, we are still witnesses to the world that the Word of God is true.

We are witnesses to the Biblical significance of healing. God heals because that is part of his nature — he is the Lord our healer (Exod. 15:26). If Jesus sought to bring healing to the sick, so should we. Even as he is a healer, so should we be healers. Jesus heals because he wishes to destroy the works of the devil (1 Jn. 3:8), of which sickness is one. God heals because he has compassion upon us, and we also are to be a people of compassion and mercy. If we have properly understood the significance of healing, we are compelled to practice it.

We are witnesses who participate in the sufferings of Christ which may come because of our following Jesus in the ministry of healing. After the paralyzed man was healed, Peter paid a price — spending the night in jail (Ac. 4:3). John Wimber was criticized and deserted by many because of his persistence in seeking God for the healing of his people. Any supernatural demonstration is bound to result in demonic backlash, because it represents a direct threat to the kingdom of darkness. Following Jesus always means walking in the way of the cross, and we had better be prepared for it before we take up the battle.

We are witnesses who pursue the practice of healing faithfully for as long as God calls us. God has not called us to say a quick prayer, then desert the person if our prayer is not immediately answered. We are called to be those who persevere to the end, no matter what the circumstances or how many times we may have felt disappointed. Who knows how often a breakthrough has been imminent just when people stopped praying? "And let us not grow weary of doing good, for in due season we will reap, if we do not give up" (Gal. 6:9). We are to be runners who finish the race. Only God can heal, and only God can bring results, but he calls us to be faithful.

FIFTH PRINCIPLE: THE IMPORTANCE OF RIGHT RELATIONSHIPS

If our relationship with God and with each other is not in a healthy place, it will be difficult for us to be agents of God's healing. Referring to the broken relationships within the body, Paul declares it is because of these that "many of you are weak and ill, and some have died" (1 Cor. 11:30). Humanity is a unity of body, soul and spirit. How we act toward God and others is the expression of our inner emotional and physical health. If we are not walking in a place of spiritual health, how can God use us to minister physical health to others? I am convinced that the lack of healing in the church in our culture, whether physical or emotional in nature, is due in considerable measure to the superficiality of our relationship with God and the brokenness of our relationships between one another. Healing will not come out of a dysfunctional body, nor will it come out of a body with superficial commitment to the lordship of Jesus Christ. In order to minister healing to a sick and broken world, we need to maintain a strong and deep relationship with the Lord and with our brothers and sisters in Christ. We want to bring those sick in body and spirit into a place of healing, which is what God's family should be. We must guard our relationships, for it is out of these relationships that we minister the life of Jesus to the world.

SIXTH PRINCIPLE: HEALING IS FOR THE WHOLE PERSON

"If on the Sabbath a man receives circumcision, so that the law of Moses may not be broken, are you angry with me because on the Sabbath I made a man's whole body well?" (Jn. 7:23). The word for "well" in this verse is *hugies*. There are three words for healing in the New Testament. The first is *therapeuo* (and related words), occurring 46 times. The second is *iaomai* (and related words), occurring 32 times. The third (and least common) is *hugies* (and its related verb), which occur 23 times. The first two words focus on the element of purely physical healing, whereas *hugies*, the least common, is much broader, including all kinds of healing and wholeness. This comes out in Paul's use of the same word where he speaks of "sound" or "healthy" doctrine and speech (1 Tim. 1:10; 2 Tim. 4:3). Paul also speaks of being "sound" or "healthy" in the faith, referring in context to people of godly character and conduct (Tit. 1:13; 2:2.). The force of the word is again emphasized in the Greek translation of the Hebrew Old Testament, where nine times *hugies* translates the Hebrew word *shalom*, which refers to the state of wholeness or peace God desires us to experience in our lives.

In his book (page 172), John Wimber added these three practical points illustrating the importance of ministering to the person as a whole:

It is more important to know *what kind of person has the illness* rather than *what kind of illness has the person.* It is helpful to know something about a person's whole relationship with God when we come to pray for them. Are we treating the symptom and ignoring the cause?

We need to remember that *we are praying for people and not simply conditions.* This keeps our focus on the mercy of Jesus toward people and on the person's dignity and worth before God. It may also increase the effectiveness of our healing ministry toward them, as we touch all the affected areas of their lives.

Our goal in praying for people is to *leave them feeling more loved by God than before they had been prayed for.* People are not objects of our ministry gifting, but the recipients of our love. Our focus in prayer is not to get results and enhance our healing ministry but to show the love of Jesus to people. By praying, we show a care which touches their hearts. Even if they are not healed, they are still touched by our care and compassion. In many years of ministry, I have never found anyone resentful at my offer to pray for them.

ESCHATOLOGY

A friend at seminary made the remark, "Your eschatology affects everything you believe." At the time I brushed his comment off. No longer. Here's why my view has changed.

The New Testament consistently asserts that the last days began with the earthly ministry of Jesus and the launch of the church at Pentecost. If you believe that the last days refer only to an immediate brief period before the return of Christ, you will not be able to understand fully the meaning of the Christian life now.

The New Testament consistently asserts that all God's promises to Abraham are fulfilled in Christ and in his body, not in the state of Israel or the Jewish people as an ethnic group. If you believe that the main prophetic program of God deals with Israel, you will fail to understand fully the meaning of God's purposes for the church.

The New Testament consistently asserts that wars and political conflicts, famines, pestilence, and natural disasters will occur throughout the church age and are not in themselves signs of the end. If you believe that such phenomena are a sign of the end, you will spend most of your time fixated on the latest news reports from the middle east and other peripheral items, you will become fear-focussed, not faith-focussed, and you will miss what God is really doing on the earth.

Now do you see how your eschatology, even if you weren't aware of it, affects everything you believe and even how you live?

HOW DID WE GET INTO THIS MESS?

In 1830, a young woman in Scotland called Margaret MacDonald had a vision concerting the events leading up to the return of Christ. She wrote these words: "Only those who have the light of God within them will see the sign of his appearance… 'tis only those that are alive in him that will be caught up to meet him in the air."

Around the same time, a Bible teacher in England called John Nelson Darby developed his doctrine of the secret rapture of the church. It has been alleged that Darby was influenced by Margaret MacDonald's vision. Darby certainly knew of her. Between 1831 and 1833, Darby held a series of prophetic conferences in which he outlined his revelation of a secret rapture to be followed by a seven year tribulation. He taught further that the kingdom of God as portrayed in the Old Testament was completely different from the church. The kingdom would be fulfilled only in a series of events commencing in the restoration of the state of Israel, which he prophesied as early as 1829. At the end of a seven-year tribulation, Christ would return to earth to establish an earthly rule based in Jerusalem. He developed a system of Biblical interpretation called dispensationalism, which divides history into ages in which God relates to people differently, the primary difference being between Israel and the church. This was a system of thought previously unknown to Christianity.

The idea of Christ's secret return was also picked up by Charles Taze Russell, founder of the Jehovah's Witnesses, who declared Christ had already invisibly returned in 1874 to begin the end-times harvest through the Jehovah's Witnesses. Russell also picked up Darby's ideas of dispensations, and further declared that the kingdom of God was established in heaven in 1914, to be governed by a group of 144,000 chosen Witnesses who would work to establish a literal paradise on earth.

In the early 1840s, William Miller, co-founder of the Seventh Day Adventists, predicted that Christ would return in 1844. When this did not happen, he declared that Christ had (invisibly to us) entered the heavenly sanctuary to commence the process of eternal judgment.

Mormonism, birthed around the same time period, though not accepting the secret rapture, endorsed Darby's concept of a literal earthly millennium.

Dispensationalism was popularized with the publication of a study Bible by C.I. Scofield, an associate of D.L. Moody, in 1909. It burst into prominence further with the apparent vindication of Darby's prophecy concerning the restoration of the state of Israel in 1948. Its view of the rapture, the secret return of Christ, the tribulation and the literal thousand year millennium was entrenched by the best-selling book *The Late Great Planet Earth* by Hal Lindsey, and by the *Left Behind* books and films of Tim LaHaye and Jerry Jenkins.

Today, this understanding of eschatology is the prevailing view among Christians in North America, even if few have comprehension of its details and consequences. Many, if not most of you reading this book have, knowingly or not, allowed your understanding of the end-times to be conditioned by it.

If that is the case, you need to know the shaky foundations of what you have accepted as true. In the following paragraphs, we list the main points of dispensationalism. After that, we'll try to show why they are wrong.

WHAT IS DISPENSATIONALISM?

According to dispensational teaching, the key to the fulfilment of all Bible prophecy regarding the end-times is the re-establishment of the state of Israel in 1948. This was necessary in order for the events of the tribulation (which focus on an attack on Israel by the Antichrist) to take place. This in turn paves the way for the re-establishment of an earthly Davidic kingdom (as promised to King David) and restoration of temple sacrifices during the millennium.

According to dispensationalist teaching, God's intention in sending Christ to earth was to fulfill God's promise to David that his descendants would rule over an eternal earthly kingdom. Unexpectedly, the Jewish people rejected God's offer and crucified the Messiah instead. God was now faced with a problem. He resorted to Plan B. He raised Jesus from the dead, and created the church. The church was not his original purpose, but exists as a "parenthesis" in the divine plan, which is still centered on Israel. God is thus left with two covenant peoples, and deals separately with each. The dispensations cannot overlap.

God must now fulfil his original plan to establish an earthly kingdom ruled over by Christ. In order to do so, while maintaining the distinction between the two covenant peoples, he must remove the church from the equation. This occurs through a secret return of Christ, visible only to the church, called the "rapture."

The rapture then precipitates the seven year tribulation allegedly prophesied in Dn. 9:24-27 and referred to in Rev. 7:14 as "the great tribulation."

The events of this tribulation are described in Revelation chapters 6 through 19. During this time, a personal Antichrist will arise. At first he appears friendly to Israel, but then betrays his agreement, and turns his attention to Israel's destruction. In the ensuing period of crisis, many of the Jewish people will be converted to faith in Christ. At the end of the tribulation, Christ will return again, this time visibly, and destroy the forces of the Antichrist at Armageddon.

Following Armageddon, Christ will establish an earthly, thousand-year rule from Jerusalem that was God's original intention. Jews (and a very few Gentiles) saved in the tribulation will enter this kingdom, and will live very long and healthy lives, many surviving right through until the end of the millennium. At the beginning of the millennium, only believers will live on the earth, the unsaved being held in Hades until the final judgment following the thousand years. It is possible that those who do die may be instantly resurrected and gain immortal bodies, existing alongside those still mortal. Raptured saints in glorified bodies meanwhile reside in the new Jerusalem, which will hover above the earth and be visible to it, but will also from time to time mingle with the mortal inhabitants of the earth. Worship will be conducted from the restored temple. The Levitical priesthood and offerings will be re-instituted as the means of worshipping God. At the end of the thousand years, a further rebellion will take place, described in Rev. 20:7-10. This is apparently led by the unsaved children of millennial believers. Christ will defeat them and merge his two kingdoms into the eternal new Jerusalem. The resurrection of the dead will at last take place, and the lost will be released from Hades and cast into the lake of fire.

Let's take this apart and examine it piece by piece.

Claim number one: The key to the fulfilment of all Bible prophecy is the re-establishment of the state of Israel in 1948. All God's end-times promises in the Old Testament were directed toward Israel, and would culminate in the establishment of an earthly kingdom led by a descendent of David. *Response:* The Bible teaches that all Old Testament prophecies are fulfilled in and through Christ and Christ alone. This is especially true of the Jewish feasts. Christ is the new temple (Jn. 2:13-22; 4:21-26). He fulfils the Sabbath (Mt. 12:1-8), the Passover (Jn. 19:36), the Day of

Atonement (Isa. 52:13-53:12) and the Feast of Tabernacles, which promised the outpouring of the Spirit (Jn. 7:37-44). Christ is the new Bethel (Jn. 1:51), the promised Messianic wine (Jer. 31:12; Jn. 2:1-12), and the new manna (Jn. 6:1-15, 30-34). He is the promised giver of abundant water and the Spirit (Ezek. 36:25-27; Jn. 3:1-15). He is the new Moses (Ac. 3:22-26), who calms the sea and walks on the water (Jn. 6:16-21). The entire Old Testament in its prophecy and typology points to Christ. If Israel was God's son (Hos. 11:1), Jesus is the true and unique Son (Mt. 2:15; Jn. 1:14) and thus also the true Israel, in that all God's promises for the nation are fulfilled in his life, death, resurrection, exaltation, session and second coming. This principle is necessarily extended to his body, the church. This is why Jesus and his body, the church, constitute the true Israel, fulfilling the promise given to Moses, "You shall be to me a kingdom of priests and a holy nation" (Exod. 19:6; applied to the church in 1 Pet. 2:9; Rev. 1:6; 5:10). Jesus, the Son of David, fulfilled the promises made to David concerning an eternal kingdom. This kingdom was initiated by Jesus in his earthly ministry and will come in its consummation at his return.

Claim number two: God sent Christ to earth to establish an earthly kingdom in Jerusalem and rule as the fulfillment of God's promise to David. Unexpectedly, the Jewish people rejected God's offer and crucified the Messiah instead. God was now faced with a problem. He resorted to Plan B. He raised Jesus from the dead and created the church. The church was never his focus, but exists as a "parenthesis" in the divine plan, which is centered instead on Israel. God thus has two covenant peoples and deals separately with each of them. *Response:* God sent Jesus into the world for one reason only: to suffer and die for our sins on the cross (Isa. 52:13-53:12; Psalm 22. God has infinite foreknowledge, and his plan from all eternity was to send Christ to earth to create one new people out of Jew and Gentile alike (Eph. 1:3-10; 2:11-22). He did this in order to fulfil the promise given to Abraham that through his offspring all the nations of the earth would be blessed (Gen. 22:18). God has only one covenant people; believing Jews are incorporated along with Gentiles into the body of Christ (Gal. 3:28-29; Eph. 4:6). The earthly Jerusalem, racial Israel, is fulfilled in the heavenly Jerusalem, the church (Gal. 4:21-31). Believing Jews represent the faithful remnant saved through faith in Christ and added to the church (Rom. (9:6-13, 11:23-32). The church is the apex of God's plan (Eph. 3:7-13).

Claim number three: God must fulfil his original plan, which was to establish an earthly kingdom ruled over by Christ, but in order to do so he must remove the church from the equation. This occurs through the secret return of Christ called the "rapture." *Response:* There is no Biblical evidence for the rapture, the so-called "secret return" of Christ. Christ described his return as visible to the entire world, saved and unsaved alike (Mt. 24:27), and never once said he would return prior to that secretly. The word "rapture" does not occur anywhere in the Bible. The primary passage cited in support is 2 Thess. 4:13-18, which describes the "appearing" (Greek *parousia*) or return of the Lord. Christians will be "caught up" in the air to "meet" the Lord at his appearing. There is no suggestion in the text that the return is visible to Christians only. The meaning of the passage is determined by the word "appearing" or "coming" (*parousia*, verse 15). This word was used to describe the visit of the Emperor to a city. The citizens would go out of the city to meet the Emperor at his "appearing." But then they would escort him back into the city where he would take up his place of rulership. Paul is describing, in highly pictorial language, how Christians will encounter Christ at his return. Far from leaving this world the opposite is true. They will *escort him back into* the eternally-renewed earth and heaven of the new Jerusalem. A second passage is Mt. 24:41, when at the Lord's coming one will be "taken" and the other "left." The context, dealing with Noah's flood, shows that the one "taken" is headed to perdition, whereas it is actually the one "left" who is saved. The last passage cited in support of the secret rapture is Rev. 3:10, where Jesus promises the church in Philadelphia he will keep them from the hour of trial (tribulation) coming on the earth. But this promise is specific to that church only, not to the other six, and its meaning is grounded in that church's first century experience of Roman persecution. Why would the Lord promise to the Philadelphians protection from an event none of them would live to see? The consistent teaching of the New Testament is that the word "tribulation" refers to the experiences of the church throughout its history, rather than being an exclusively end-times phenomenon. The word used in Rev. 3:10 is not even the normal word for "tribulation" (Greek *thlipsis*) but rather the word "testing" (Greek *peirasmos*). On the "great tribulation" see further below.

Claim number four: The rapture precipitates the seven-year tribulation prophesied by Daniel and mentioned in Rev. 7:14. *Response:* (1) This claim is based on a twisted interpretation of Dn. 9:24-27. Daniel prophesies a period of time specified as seventy weeks (seventy times seven) commencing in the decree of Cyrus in 538 BC allowing the Jews to return to Jerusalem. Prophetic numbers in the Bible are always symbolic, and this is no exception. The land has just completed its seventy years (seven times ten) which Scripture identifies as a Sabbath rest. The purpose of the 490 weeks is to provide forgiveness (verse 24). In other words, it is an escalation of the year of Jubilee (seven times seven years), the year all debts were forgiven. The year of Jubilee is the final forgiveness of sins in Christ. The attaining of ultimate forgiveness in the escalated Jubilee is followed by the destruction of Jerusalem (verses 26b and 27b), also prophesied by Jesus. The Messiah will die (v 26a) but following his death will put an end to the sacrificial system (verse 27a). Nowhere in this is there any hint of a literal seven year period of tribulation. (2) Use of the word "tribulation" in Revelation and the New Testament does not refer to an end-times phenomenon but to the experience of the entire church age. The phrase "the great tribulation" occurs in Rev. 7:14, where it speaks of the vast multitude of saints who have died and entered the presence of the Lord, having endured the trials of the present church age. The four other occurrences of the word "tribulation" (Greek *thlipsis*) in Revelation refer to events of the present church age (1:9; 2:9; 2:10; 2:22). Jesus uses the word the same way (Jn. 16:33), as does Luke (Ac. 14:22). Twenty-one out of twenty-three occurrences of the word in Paul refer clearly to present reality (Rom. 5:3; 8:35-36; 2 Tim. 3:12, etc.). The New Testament connects the idea of tribulation with the sufferings of this present time. "The great tribulation" is the church age.

Claim number five: The events of this tribulation are described in Revelation chapters 6 through 19. During this time a personal Antichrist will arise to oppose Israel. In the ensuing persecution, many of the Jewish people will be converted to faith in Christ. Christ will return a second time, visibly, and destroy the forces of the Antichrist at Armageddon. *Response:* The events of Revelation 6-19 do not commence at the very end of history following the rapture. They commence at the ascension of Christ to the right hand of God (Revelation 5). Christ unseals the book given to him (Rev. 6:1) *and from that very moment* releases a series of judgments described in chapters 6-20 which continue throughout the church age. The entire church age is described in various ways in the visions of chapters 6-20. The last battle is alluded to five times in Revelation at the end of each series of judgments, all of which describe the same set of events (6:12-17; 11:13; 14:14-20; 16:17-21, continued in 19:11-21; 20:7-10). The visions are like the gospels, which describe the same period of history from different perspectives. John records the visions as he sees them. Some go back in time prior to preceding visions. Armageddon is not a literal place, but is a symbolic reference to the places throughout the world where the enemy attacks the worldwide church at the end of the church age, and is ended by the visible return of Christ. The "camp of the saints" (Rev. 20:9) attacked by the devil and his forces at the end of the millennium is not Israel but the church; the word "saints" appears thirteen times elsewhere in Revelation and every time refers to all believers, Jew and Gentile alike (5:8; 13:7-10. 14:12, etc.). After Christ's only and visible return comes the resurrection of the just and unjust, the Great White Throne judgment and the advent of the new Jerusalem, the eternal kingdom (Rev. 20:11-15).

Claim number six: Following Armageddon, Christ will establish his earthly rule from Jerusalem that was God's original intention. Jews saved in the tribulation will enter it and live very long lives, quite possibly surviving right through until the end of the millennium. It is possible, however, though not certain, that those who do die may be instantly resurrected and gain immortal bodies. Raptured saints in glorified bodies meanwhile reside in the new Jerusalem, which will hover above the earth, but will also mingle with the mortal inhabitants on the earth. Worship will be conducted from the restored temple. The Levitical priesthood and offerings will be re-instituted as the means of worshipping God. At the end of the millennium there will occur a further rebellion led by unsaved children of millennial believers. Christ will defeat them and merge his two kingdoms into the eternal new Jerusalem. *Response:* The description of the battle in 20:7-10, which occurs at the end of the millennium, shows it is identical to the battle of Armageddon, described in chapters 16 and 19. This shows that the millennium, which occurs *prior to* the battle of 20:7-10, is identical to the church age, which even dispensationalists admit occurs prior to Armageddon. The Bible nowhere teaches any more than one return of Christ. The Bible clearly teaches only one resurrection of the dead. The Bible clearly teaches that the sacrifices of the law are once and for all done away with by the sacrifice of Christ. Dispensationalism teaches (1) that the curse of death on humanity and on he natural creation will continue *after Christ's second coming,* (2) that unbelievers will have the opportunity of coming to Christ *after his second coming,* and (3) that unbelievers will not be resurrected or judged *until 1000 years after Christ's second coming.* Such teachings are completely contrary to what is taught anywhere else in the New Testament.

WHY IS DISPENSATIONALISM
SO DAMAGING?

It takes the focus away from the cross of Christ and turns the clock back to the sacrifices of the law.

It takes the focus away from God's people joined from every nation, places it back on Israel and divides his purposes for Jews and Gentiles. It rebuilds the dividing wall of partition taken down by Christ.

It gives the political state of Israel a place reserved for the covenant people of God. It denies Paul's teaching on the heavenly Jerusalem.

It causes people to interpret the Bible from news reports rather than interpreting the Bible by itself, thus ignoring the more than 500 allusions in Revelation's 404 verses to the Old Testament.

It makes Revelation irrelevant for anyone except those living in the last years before the "rapture."

It teaches falsely that God's people will be saved from tribulation.

It produces fear and an obsessive focus on what may happen next in the politics of the Middle East.

And finally, it has produced hundreds of false predictions

concerning political events, the Antichrist, 666, the mark of the beast and the date of the rapture that have collectively drawn Christianity into discredit with the watching world. Very rarely has any dispensationalist repented concerning these false prophecies.

WHAT ARE THE LAST DAYS?

So much of this could have been avoided had we understood what the Bible teaches about the last days.
Eschatology comes from the Greek word *eschatos*, meaning "last." Eschatology is the study of the last things or the end times.

That is where the trouble starts. Most of us grew up, as described at length above, with the understanding that the end times were a very short period of time immediately before the return of the Lord. *But that is completely contrary to what the New Testament teaches.*

Revelation starts by quoting words from Dn. 2:44 referring to things that would happen in the "latter days." God "showed" the king things that would happen in the latter days (Dn. 2:28). These things were then "sealed up," according to Dn. 12:9, until the time of the end. John quotes Daniel's words in Rev. 1:1, 19, saying that God has also "shown him" what is to take place. But there is a significant alteration. God shows John that the things that were to take place in

Daniel's "latter days" are now to occur "shortly" or "quickly." John deliberately uses the words of Daniel to emphasize the fact that *Daniel's future is now present,* and that the events prophesied long ago *are now commencing.*

Daniel spoke of momentous events in the distant future. In the latter days, the fourth earthly kingdom of his vision would be shattered by the rock of the kingdom of God (Dn. 2:44). This coming of the kingdom is connected with the appearance of the "Son of man" who will rule over it (Dn. 7:13-14). In the vision of chapters 4 and 5, John sees these prophesied events as fulfilled in the death and resurrection of Jesus Christ. He is the Son of man prophesied in Daniel 7, and he has been exalted to the right hand of God to receive an eternal kingdom. Jesus himself interprets Daniel's rock as fulfilled in his own ministry (Lk. 20:18). The latter days to Daniel were a future far-off and whose secrets were to be sealed until the end time (Dn. 12:9). To John, however, it is something *about to unfold before his eyes.*

The events prophesied by Daniel have begun to occur, set in motion by the death and resurrection of Christ. All that is about to happen – from the events occurring in the seven churches of Asia to the events which will occur as the rest of the church age unfolds – are now being unsealed or revealed, which is what Revelation is all about. The "latter days" are indeed at hand, about to happen quickly, in the same sense that Jesus said the kingdom of heaven was at hand or about to arrive (Mk. 1:15). It is no longer for a distant future, but is right in front of us, about to happen. The visions John is about to unfold represent events which will begin to occur almost immediately, and will continue until Jesus returns. *The last days are now.*

If this seems strange to us, consider this. In Ac. 2:17-21, Peter declares that at Pentecost the "last days" prophesied by Joel have begun, and he moves immediately and seamlessly in interpreting Joel as announcing both Pentecost (verses 17-19), and (without apparent time delay) the prophesied day of the Lord (the last judgment) in verses 19-21. Thus he collapses all of history after Christ into the category of the last days, and declares we are living in them. A similar understanding of the last days is found in Hebrews ("In these last days he has spoken to us by his Son," 1:2), James ("You have laid up treasure in the last days," 5:3), and Peter ("[He] was made manifest in the last times," 1 Pet.1:20). John elsewhere interprets it this way himself: "Children, it is the last hour" (1 Jn. 2:18). The Bible understands the last days to be the days commencing with the death and resurrection of Christ and concluding with his return. This time period – otherwise known as the church age – is the age in which John lived and the age in which we still live, and it is this age which is described in the visions which unfold from Rev. 6:1 onwards.

Why are the last days now? Because the kingdom is present now. We are in the very last phase of human history. God measures time differently than we do. A thousand years is as a day in his sight.

Daniel (chapter 7) saw Jesus in a vision approaching the throne of God. John sees exactly the same vision in Revelation chapter 5. Daniel saw a book which was sealed up until the time of the end. John saw Jesus taking that very book and unsealing it at the moment of his ascension to the right hand of God. All the rest of the events recorded in Revelation commence at Jesus' ascension when the book is unsealed. Those events were already occurring in the life of the seven churches to whom John wrote, and they continue to occur today. They revolve around a series of judgments involving the powers of darkness which are both permitted and used by God for his sovereign purposes. When neither the church nor the world is listening to God through the preaching of his Word, God takes his hand off his merciful restraint and allows the church and the world to see a glimpse of what it deserves. God has two goals in mind: to call a complacent church back to himself, and to warn a rebellious world that if it does not pay heed to the judgments it is suffering it will face a far worse judgment in the future. The judgments are undoubtedly intended by the enemy for evil and harm, yet God turns them to a good purpose. He never intended sickness or death to invade this world. That is our responsibility. But he turns even the worst things to good.

So the wars, earthquakes, famine and pestilence Jesus prophesied (Lk. 21:9-11) are actually not signs of the very end, but are characteristic of the entire age from his ascension to his return. He makes a sharp difference between these occurrences and the powers of the heavens being shaken (Lk. 21:26, depicted also in the sixth seal, trumpet and bowl judgment), which will cause us to realize our redemption is near. Yet even then, no one knows the hour, not even the Son, but only the Father (Mk. 13:32).

So there is an end times, and there is also an "end of the end times." The same thing is pictured in Revelation. The first four or five sets of judgments pertain to the whole church age, and the sixth and seventh portray the very end and the arrival of God's eternal kingdom.

THE MESSAGE OF REVELATION IS FOR US TODAY

If all this is the case, then the words written in Revelation are *as relevant for us today as they were when John wrote them and as they will be until Christ returns.* Dispensationalism has destroyed this Biblical messaging through its obsessive focus on the restoration of the state of Israel. Revelation has over 500 allusions to the Old Testament in its 404 verses, more allusions than every other book of the New Testament combined. It must be interpreted by these references. One of the controlling images of Revelation is the idea of a second Exodus. Believers are portrayed as delivered from spiritual Egypt, protected in a threatening wilderness for the duration of the church age, and having the assurance they will be ushered safely into the Promised Land of the New Jerusalem. The 42 months, three and a half years or 1260 days the church spends in the wilderness (Rev. 11:3; 12:6, 15; 13:5) represents the 42 years Moses and Israel spent in the wilderness, during which there were 42 encampments, and the 42 months Elijah spent in the desert.

We live in the "in-between," in that place where the kingdom has broken in but is not yet reached its perfect form, where we suffer for our faith yet are spiritually protected, where we experience the power of God even as we walk in human weakness. That period of the "in-between" is referred to as both the "great tribulation" and the "millennium." These are present, not future realities.

Revelation, properly understood, has three major pastoral and theological messages for us as believers now:

1. The way of the cross is the path to eternal victory. The cross was the foundation of Christ's victory over Satan. Christians are called to follow in Christ's footsteps. The sufferings of believers in this present age assure their victory over the powers of darkness. We suffer hardship now (1:9), but will share later in Christ's kingly rule (1:6). Our spirit will be kept safe in the midst of physical suffering (11:1-7). By contrast, though unbelievers presently carry out evil acts (11:10), these acts serve only to form the basis for their final judgment (11:13, 18). One of the main purposes of Revelation is to exhort believers to remain faithful in the face of adversity in the assurance of final victory. The focus of Revelation is *ethical*, not predictive, as is indicated by the exhortations in the first and last chapters to obey the words of this prophecy (1:3; 22:7). The prophetic exhortation is to maintain a lifestyle loyal to Christ and free from the idolatry of the surrounding pagan culture.

2. God is sovereign over human history. The visionary section of the book is introduced by the vision of the throne room of God and the Lamb in chapters 4 and 5. In these chapters, the word "throne," signifying God's sovereignty, appears seventeen times. This vision demonstrates the authority of God and of the Lamb over all that is about to unfold in the book's remainder. God the Father and Jesus identify themselves respectively at the book's beginning and end as the "Alpha and the Omega," the Lord of the beginning, the Lord of the end, and the Lord of everything in between. The trials of believers, the apparent victory of the enemy, the eventual destruction of the latter and victory of the church, are all under the sovereign control of God.

3. The history which began in the first Garden-temple ends in the Garden-temple of the new Jerusalem. The new Jerusalem is the fulfillment of God's plan to establish a garden-like paradise. Adam, commissioned as a priest, failed in his commission to extend the boundaries of the original Garden-temple. Israel likewise failed in her commission to be a light to the nations. But Christ succeeded where Adam and Israel failed. The boundaries of the kingdom extend throughout the earth in the church age, though only in an imperfect manner. Before the Lord returns, the gospel of the kingdom will reach every nation (Mt. 24:14). But in the new Jerusalem, the Garden is perfectly established forever. The serpent, allowed into the first Garden, is cast out of the last Garden. All God's expressions of covenant with men and women are fulfilled as they worship him in the final, perfect Garden-temple. This is the story line of the Bible.

And now maybe you understand why eschatology matters.

MONEY

Let me start with a statement that may surprise or even shock you: "Jesus talked much about money. Sixteen of the thirty-eight parables were concerned with how to handle money and possessions. In the Gospels, an amazing one out of ten verses (288 in all) deal directly with the subject of money. The Bible offers 500 verses on prayer, less than 500 verses on faith, but more than 2,000 verses on money and possessions" (Howard L. Dayton, writing in Leadership magazine). Dr. Larry Burkett, author of many books on finance and stewardship, compiled a 280 page volume simply listing all those verses.

The fact is that our use of money is about the most reliable external indicator of where our heart is. Where would I get such an idea from? From the man who said: "For where your treasure is, there will your heart be also" (Mt. 6:21).

And also from the man who inserted mention of Christ's sacrifice of his own life right into the middle of a discussion about money: "Though he was rich, yet for your sake he became poor, so that you by his poverty might become rich" (2 Cor. 8:9).

So why is it that we rarely talk about money in church?

Where then do we start? Maybe by saying that money in itself is not bad. People who think this is so often misquote the Bible as saying: "Money is the root of all evil things." Actually, what Paul wrote to Timothy was this: "For the love of money is a root of all kinds of evil" (1 Tim. 6:10). Money is neutral. It's what we do with it that matters.

And that is exactly why God established the tithe. Don't get angry because I'm temporarily changing the conversation from money to giving. Just bear with me for a moment and you'll see where I'm going.

God established the tithe for one main reason: *to enable us to acknowledge that he is the rightful owner of everything we have, and to acknowledge that all our wealth and prosperity comes from him.* Most Christians don't tithe anyway, but even those who do generally believe that as long as we give to God his share, we can do what we want with the rest and expect he will bless it. That's not true. The tithe tells us that it all belongs to him. Jacob understood this, which was why he said: "And of all that you give me I will give you a tenth" (Gen. 28:22). If we acknowledge that God owns all we have, it is no longer a big issue to tithe. But if we don't acknowledge that, it becomes difficult to give anything at all. That's why Christians are often divided into two groups — those who tithe and those who fall very far short of tithing, often giving only nominal amounts. *The issue is not the percentage we give, the issue is where our hearts are at.* If our hearts are right, the percentages sort themselves out. And so do our bank balances, because it is usually those who fall short in their giving who have financial difficulties, not those who tithe. We'll find out why before we finish.

The tithe therefore establishes the fact that God is the owner of everything we possess, and that we are only stewards. God created this world and along with it the potential for creation of material wealth. It all ultimately belongs to him, and ultimately he will take it all back. That, and not worship of Gaia or Greenpeace, is the basis for a Christian ecology. If you doubt that God is the owner and we are the stewards of his wealth, consider the parable of the talents. Of course it involves more than money, but you can't spiritualize out of it the fact that Jesus chose to use handling of money as a symbol for how we handle everything else in life.

MONEY AND THE KINGDOM OF GOD

So may I suggest that the first thing you need in order to manage your money properly is an understanding of the kingdom of God. You need to understand what God is doing in the world he created in order to line up your resources with his priorities. Common sense tells you that if you line your life up with the Creator of all wealth it might actually be good for your bank account.

Listen to the words of Jesus: "Seek first the kingdom of God and his righteousness, and all these things will be added to you" (Mt. 6:33). In this verse, Jesus gives a clear definition of God's purposes for our lives on earth. We are here to seek the establishment of his kingdom. It is very significant that Jesus makes this statement *in the context of teaching on finance.* He has instructed his disciples not to lay up treasures on earth (verse 20). He has told them they cannot serve God and money (verse 24). He has urged them to stop worrying about how they will have their needs met (verses 25-32). Jesus has money in mind! The essence of verse 33, therefore, is that we are to give ourselves to God's kingdom, and he will take care of all our financial needs. No one more completely modeled this way of life than Jesus himself.

If we do not have an understanding of God's purposes on earth and how we fit into them, we will never have a motivation for submitting our finances to him. If we do not see that God has a purpose for our lives and that he commands us to put all our priorities at his disposal, we will never understand his claim on our finances or any other part of our lives. We will never see that how we handle money is of any concern to God at all. God may be concerned about our sexual morality, but money? Why would he be interested in that? But that is a problem, once we have determined that all of our wealth has been created by God, and merely loaned to us to steward on his behalf during our earthly life. God is our Provider - that is one of his names. *But to access his provision our finances must be under his control.*

How do we know that our finances are under his control? The best sign is that we are handling our resources the way God manages his. All of God's purposes are based on the concept of giving. God is a giver. God gave us the whole creation to steward and enjoy. Even though we abused his trust in this, he gave us his Son to restore us to relationship with him. No one practiced giving more consistently than Jesus. He spent his whole life doing nothing but giving. Now he calls us to follow in his footsteps. Christians are those who are always looking to give of their time and resources. They don't worry about who is going to give back to them, for they have already found their own source of provision in their relationship with the Lord. Anything else that comes back from others is an unexpected bonus.

But the amazing thing is that the more people you give away to, the more God comes and restores to you, and the more he gives back to you through others, even when you're not looking for it. It is through the giving of our time and resources that his kingdom is extended.

THE IDOLATRY OF DEBT

How do we know that our finances are out of control? In one word: debt. God never envisioned that his people would be in debt. If someone did fall into dire poverty in ancient Israel, it was expected that others would help them out. Loans were not loans in our sense, in that they carried no interest (Exod. 22:25) and were to be forgiven every seventh year (Deut. 15:1-2). People always had the option of becoming someone's servant, in which case they were responsible for looking after you properly and meeting all your needs in return for your service.

Our modern society is swimming in a sea of debt. It has become almost impossible for Christians to avoid it. But just because we cannot avoid it does not mean we have to embrace it.

Debt is rooted in idolatry. We want something that God has not seen fit to provide for us, and we violate his principles in order to get it. If our treasure is truly in heaven, we can rest content with what God has provided materially and be grateful for it. If our joy is in Christ, we do not need it to be supplemented by the accumulation of possessions we might like to have but do not actually need. Sadly, we live in a consumerist culture where happiness is measured in part by the stuff we own and by comparison to the stuff others own.

In previous generations, we would have had to do without. The first true credit cards did not come into operation until about fifty years ago. Prior to that there was only American Express, but that was for the convenience of business travellers so they didn't have to carry mountains of cash with them, and it had to be paid off at the end of every month. You could get a mortgage and a car loan, but that was about it. Now we use credit cards to buy everything, and a significant number of people never quite manage to pay them off. The interest charges accumulate and drive people into bankruptcy. As soon as they get out of it, they start all over again.

None of this makes any financial sense. But neither does it make Biblical sense. And this is why. If we believe that God supplies our needs, then to make living on credit a lifestyle makes it clear we believe that God has not supplied what we needed and we must supplement it. It's the same attitude the Israelites had when they got tired of the boring and mundane manna, and began to yearn for the exotic food of Egypt. To live this way becomes a form of idolatry.

THE PROBLEM WITH THE PROSPERITY MESSAGE

This highlights the basic problem with the so-called prosperity message. It caters to our desire for more and more stuff by using prayer to get what we want from God. It betrays an attitude of the heart that is wrong, and wrong in more than one way.

First, it shows that we are all too deeply rooted in the desire for the things of this world. It shows a dissatisfaction with what the Lord has provided us. And second, it is a form of attempted manipulation of God. The prosperity message is an aspect of the word of faith teaching (see chapter on faith), and is guilty of the same charges levelled against that.

Though they declare their allegiance to the concept of divine prosperity, people who fall into this trap are often affected by what I call a poverty spirit. How can a prosperity message go with a poverty spirit? Let me explain.

BREAKING THE POVERTY SPIRIT

In 2 Corinthians chapters 8 and 9, Paul deals with the crucial impact our attitude toward money has on our relationship with the Lord. He sets the stage by reminding the Corinthians of the attitude of Christ, who "though he was rich, yet for your sake he became poor, so that you by his poverty might become rich" (2 Cor. 8:9). This emphasizes the point we made above: *God is a giver.* God is a giver because he has no needs. He lives in an infinite abundance, and loves nothing more than to give generously. We became rich because of what Christ gave to us. *When God brings people into his kingdom, his desire is that they become like him.* Good managers will handle their master's finances the same way the master would — not by hoarding, but by giving, not by selfishness, but by generosity, not by accumulating, but by investing, not by focussing on enriching themselves, but planning how they can use resource to further the kingdom. As long as we do this, God himself will give us more seed to sow than what we have given: "And God is able to make all grace abound to you, so that having all sufficiency in all things at all times, you may abound in every good work" (2 Cor. 9:8). God wants a people who live in an *assurance of supply.* We are to become like Christ, who gave everything for us – yet in returning to the Father wound up with as much as he ever began with.

Fallen human nature, on the other hand, operates out of a *mentality of need.* It defines us as people who never have enough. Even though Adam and Eve lived in an unbelievable measure of prosperity and had all they needed, they did not believe it. The serpent succeeded in focussing Eve's attention on the one thing she did not have. This establishes a second point: *fallen men and women are takers.* No matter how much we have (certainly in comparison with those in poorer nations), rarely are we content with our present situation. A poverty spirit or mentality of need is never satisfied (Prov. 30:15-16). John D. Rockefeller was the richest man in the United States, yet when asked what was the best million he had ever made, gave the answer: "The next million."

The prosperity message is especially attractive to people who feel they do not have enough — people with a poverty spirit. Instead of being content with what God has given, they look around and see others with more. This births a sense of dissatisfaction. They are then taught that their apparent poverty has been caused by lack of faith, and can only be overcome by asking God in faith for as much or more than their wealthier neighbor has. This causes them to overlook legitimate reasons why their finances may not be in order, such as unwise spending, debt and so on. Faith becomes like a spiritual credit card. You can run up the bill as much as you want and ask God to pay it. Instead of dealing with the root problems of envy, materialism and poor stewardship, the prosperity message suggests that God will give you what you want. But of course he doesn't. And you're left with a wrecked faith and a load of bills.

God wants a people who have moved from a *mentality of need* to an *assurance of supply.* Paul learned to be content with whatever God provided, whether a lot or a little (Phil.

4:11-12). He knew God would supply all his needs, and went on to say so a few verses later (Phil. 4:19). People who think they are poor (regardless of their actual income) will never have a healthy, Biblical attitude toward money. They will be tightfisted and stingy. They will dwell in self-pity. They will be continuously fearful of financial disaster. They will underestimate what they have and overestimate what others have, and then be envious of those they think have more. They will feel the world owes them, and will be ungrateful to God for what he has provided. Whatever they receive is never enough. They will never be able to give generously, and will always be thinking of what they are having to do without because of what they have given. And when they are presented with teaching that tells them they can have whatever they want if only they ask in faith, they fall right into it head-first. And then the disillusionment sets in, because God will not be manipulated. The cause of the disillusionment was not God's failure to provide, but the fact they believed an illusion about God to begin with.

KINGDOM WEALTH-GENERATORS

God has a financial plan for our lives, and he is committed to providing everything we need to fulfill it. But God's will is different for each person. So is the degree to which he releases finance. Jesus clearly taught that some receive one talent, some two and some five (Mt. 25:14-30). Do not be drawn into comparisons between how much someone else has and how much you have. Rejoice in the abundance God has given to your friend. And for those who have abundance, know that God requires a more severe accounting from you for what he has entrusted to you *not* to possess, but to *steward* for his glory and kingdom. God has set different tasks before each person, and those tasks require different resources. He expects a far greater material harvest from the one with five talents than the one with only one. Having a lot of money is like handling nuclear materials: it can be toxic and spiritually life-threatening. Severe warnings are given to the rich in Jas. 4:13-5:6. Jesus said it was harder for a rich man to enter the kingdom of heaven than a camel to go through a needle, yet added that nothing was impossible with God (Mt. 19:23-26).

I believe that some are trusted with wealth by God in order to generate finances for the kingdom. It is not an easy call. Yet often God's work has been financed by such people. C.T. Studd's father was a kingdom wealth generator. His son proceeded to give away a fortune which established Christian missions and institutions around the world. Kingdom wealth generators may have nicer houses and cars than most of us. That's not the point. It's part of the world God has called them to live in. What is important, and what is often not seen, is the money that flows through their hands to the work of God. We could do with more such people, not less.

SOME SIMPLE STEPS TO TAKE

So what are we to do? Building our lives on a firm financial foundation starts with the ability to rejoice in what God has given and learn to live with it. It means refusing to go beyond what he has provided into a fantasy world which can be as damaging in terms of addiction as its sexual equivalent. It means decisively rejecting the quick fix of easy gains. Prov. 13:11 tells us the best form of wealth is that which comes through gradual accumulation. Why? Because we need deeper character in order to handle greater wealth without it drawing us away from God. And character takes time — a lot of time — to develop. In the case of what I have called kingdom wealth-generators, God gives a special grace to hold money lightly without its possession becoming spiritually destructive.

If we can see that our handling of money is a deeply spiritual issue that affects our walk with God, we might be motivated to look at it a lot more closely than often we do.

So if we are floundering in debt, what do we do? Seek good financial counselling. Get rid of debt, starting with the highest interest loans and working your way down. As more money becomes available, you can pay even more debt off.

Don't go over your head in car loans. Buy a cheaper car.

Cars are depreciating assets. The best debt, if there is such a thing, is a mortgage (which by the way means "death-grip"!), because houses generally appreciate in value. For some people, renting will be a better option, especially until they clear other debts.

And yes, give the first part of your income to God, not what's left over. I'm not saying that because I've been a pastor. I'm saying it because I want to see your finances prosper in the right way.

I wish I had a dollar for every time someone had protested, "But tithing is old covenant." No, it isn't. Let me prove it.

"THIS IS THE POINT HE TALKS ABOUT TITHING" - YES, BUT PLEASE LISTEN

Please do not think this whole discussion has been a pretext for talking about tithing. But please do not think that tithing is irrelevant to the rest of the discussion. As we pointed out at the beginning, the issue is ownership. Do we come to God as owners or as stewards?

Many people have struggled with tithing because they see it as part of the old covenant, not the new. They are mistaken. Let me show you how tithing, and the attitude of stewardship behind it, will change your finances and may change your life. You need to know these three truths.

The tithe is permanent, not temporary. One of the most common misconceptions about the tithe is that it originated in the Mosaic law, and is therefore now abolished (though the law is not so much abolished as it is fulfilled). But the tithe did not originate with the Mosaic law at all. It was instituted when Melchizedek received the tithe from Abraham (Gen. 14:20). Abraham is identified by the New Testament not as the giver of the law, but as the *father of faith for all believers in Christ.* Malachi (3:10-12) prophesied a restoration of the tithe in the coming day of the Lord. Not only that, the tithe was endorsed by the Lord Jesus himself (Lk. 11:42; Mt. 23:23-24). There is no evidence in the Bible that the tithe has been abolished for New Testament believers. But even if we did take the position that the tithe was no longer applicable, we would have to admit that the new covenant requirements on our finances, if anything, must be *more profoundly all-encompassing* than under the old covenant. Why is it that arguments that the tithe is not applicable today always seem to be justifying the idea of giving *less*, rather than *more* than believers did under the law of Moses? If the tithe is abolished, then at the least all believers should be giving *a minimum of* ten per cent, and preferably more.

The tithe originated with Christ, not Moses. We could in fact argue that the tithe originated with Christ himself.

It was Melchizedek to whom Abraham, the father of believers in Christ, tithed. And the New Testament defines Melchizedek in the following terms: king of righteousness, king of peace, without father or mother, without genealogy, without beginning of days or end of life, like the Son of God (Heb. 7:2-3). It is clear that Melchizedek cannot be a human figure. He must be either an angel, like those who appeared to Abraham and other Old Testament figures or, far more likely in light of the description given of him, a pre-incarnate manifestation of Christ himself. Did Christ really appear in the Old Testament times? Almost all Bible scholars feel he did. It is written that three angels appeared to Abraham (Gen. 18:1-33), yet one of them is identified as "the Lord." Was not the "Lord" really Christ himself, as God the Father never appears in visible bodily form? It is interesting that it was also after a visitation of angels and of "the Lord," whom Jacob saw visibly (Gen. 28:13), that he paid the tithe. Was this not also Christ and his angels? And what about the "angel of the Lord" who appeared to Moses in the burning bush (Exod. 3:2)? The angel is almost immediately redefined as "the Lord." And then "the Lord" is described as looking at Moses while at the same moment "God" speaks out of the bush (verse 4). Moses encountered both Father and Son on that incredible day! Melchizedek, then, the king of righteousness and of peace, is surely Christ himself.

It is true that under the Mosaic covenant, detailed regulations were given for the application of the tithe in the national life of Israel. The application may be somewhat different under the new covenant (in that literal priests and Levites do not exist) in the same way its use was different in the days *before* Moses. But whatever be the application, it cannot be considered abolished under the new covenant, because it was not instituted under the old. It was timeless in nature, and related from the beginning to Christ and to faith. This is confirmed by Malachi's prophetic sayings linking the new covenant in Christ not with the *abolition* of tithing, but with its *restoration*. And when we remember that according to Romans 4 Abraham is the father not just of the Jews but of all believers in Christ, what we have is this: *the tithe was birthed in a supernatural encounter between the father of all believers in Jesus and Jesus himself.* How can anyone say that is old covenant?

The tithe is thus linked with the power of an endless life. If Melchizedek is indeed Christ, then from the beginning the tithe was meant to be presented to One who is without beginning of days or end of life, *One who held within him the power of endless life.* Under the old covenant, the people presented their tithe to the Levites, and the Levites in turn presented their tithe to the priests, who in turn made their offerings to God. The ultimate result was that God responded by giving his blessing to his people (Deut. 26:15). Under the new covenant, though our tithe is presented literally to the leaders of the church, in reality it is presented to Christ, and is only stewarded by the church leadership. If we present our tithe to Christ, then Christ, as our High Priest, in turn presents it to the Father, and the Father will respond with blessing. Jesus is our High Priest in the order of Melchizedek (Heb. 7:11), and that passage ends by telling us that he comes before the Father on our behalf to intercede for us (Heb. 7:25). It is not hard for us to do anything which has life involved in it. To tithe should not be hard when we see that it releases the endless life and power of God into our lives and our finances. Do you want to plug your finances directly into the power of everlasting life? Or would you rather save a few dollars and manage them yourself?

This is not prosperity teaching. It is kingdom teaching. Seek *first* the kingdom, and all these things will be added. Try it — you might be surprised what happens.

THE BAPTISM OF
THE HOLY SPIRIT

For decades, arguments have raged among believers about the nature of the baptism of the Holy Spirit. To what exactly does it refer? What is the evidence a person has received it? What is its purpose? And how does it relate to speaking in tongues?

What I am about to share may not fit neatly into some of the well-established positions on this subject, but if it's necessary to upset apple carts in order to restore Biblical truth, I am willing to take the risk involved.

All I ask is that you carefully follow the Biblical evidence

I am going to present, and don't drop out of the discussion until I'm done.

SALVATION AND THE KINGDOM IN THE MINISTRY OF JESUS

Here is where the argument begins. Pentecostals and some charismatics say that the first disciples were genuinely saved, but did not receive the Holy Spirit until Pentecost. The baptism of the Spirit is therefore an experience received subsequent to conversion. Let's look at the evidence.

Jesus' baptism constituted the moment at which people began to move from life under the old covenant into the life of the kingdom, and that life of the kingdom above all brought salvation. Under the empowering of the Spirit, Jesus announced the arrival of the kingdom of God and the salvation long expected by the Jewish people: "The Law and the Prophets were until John; since then the good news of the kingdom is preached, and everyone forces his way into it" (Lk. 16:16). Not only did Jesus proclaim the kingdom, he appointed others to declare it also. He sent out the twelve to "proclaim the kingdom of God and to heal" (Lk. 9:2). He then sent out seventy-two more with the commission: "Heal the sick in it and say to them, 'The kingdom of God has come near to you'" (Lk. 10:9). At the very heart of Jesus' ministry was the offering of forgiveness and restoration to

God, as the parables of the lost sheep, lost coin and prodigal son illustrate (Lk. 15:1-32).

In the synagogue at Nazareth, Jesus announced the arrival of the liberation of Israel promised in Isaiah 61: "He has sent me to proclaim liberty to the captives and recovering of sight to the blind, to set at liberty those who are oppressed" (Lk. 4:18). The healings Jesus performs are therefore signs that the Messiah has come and is starting to bring liberation from oppression. When the messengers came from John the Baptist asking if Jesus is the One to come, his response was to heal "many people of diseases and plagues and evil spirits, and on many who were blind he bestowed sight" (Lk. 7:21). It is clear that already in his earthly ministry Jesus was not only declaring the kingdom, but gathering people into that kingdom through signs, wonders and healings, and through the proclamation of the Gospel message. How much more, then, must this be true of his disciples? Though many deserted him, the eleven, plus an unspecified number of other men and women, stuck with Jesus and were still there in Jerusalem awaiting the outpouring of the Spirit in Acts 1.

There is no clear line drawn between the faith of the disciples before or after Pentecost. By the time Jesus was raised but before the Spirit was poured out, they had been taught for 40 days regarding the things of the kingdom of God (Ac. 1:3). Meanwhile they were no doubt passing on this teaching to the wider group of 120, who were "devoting themselves to prayer"

(Ac. 1:14) and awaiting the promise of the Spirit. From this we draw the conclusion that the disciples and those gathered with them entered the kingdom of God long before the day of Pentecost. Pentecost was not the arrival of salvation or the kingdom, it was *a new manifestation of the kingdom which had already come.* Pentecost was exactly as Luke himself put it, the continuation of "all that Jesus began to do and teach, until the day when he was taken up" (Ac. 1:1).

Jesus did not receive the Spirit at his baptism as a first experience of God's knowledge or presence, which after all he had known from birth. Jesus received the Spirit at his baptism as the empowering from the Father to bring the kingdom to Israel. Even as by the Spirit Jesus brought God's reign to Israel during his earthly ministry, so by the Spirit the disciples will bring God's reign to Israel (and beyond) after Pentecost. In this sense, the disciples were already saved, but were awaiting the empowering of the Spirit. They experienced salvation from sin and the life of the kingdom long before they received the outpouring the Spirit.

Yet the disciples did in fact experience the reality of the Holy Spirit. The twelve and the seventy-two experienced the anointing of the Spirit when they were sent out to preach the Gospel and heal the sick. To accept Jesus and submit to him was to submit to the authority of the Spirit who empowered him. He told his followers that God would give the Holy Spirit to those who asked him (Lk. 11:11-

13), teaching something he presents as a present reality, not something to take effect after Pentecost. He taught them "through the Holy Spirit" (Ac. 1:3) for forty days after his resurrection. They did not have to experience Pentecost in order to taste life in the Spirit, for they encountered the Spirit through the ministry of Jesus. But Pentecost would bring about a different level of encounter and empowering.

In Lk. 24:44-46 and Ac. 1:2-4, Jesus prepared the disciples for the outpouring of the Spirit. By the beginning of Acts, the disciples had experienced salvation and the kingdom of God, and they had reached a full understanding of the work of Christ in his ministry and his death and resurrection. In other words, they had reached full Christian faith. What they were waiting was the prophesied empowering of the Spirit. In this sense, Pentecost is an empowering for mission to people who already are saved. Luke paints a deliberate parallel. Jesus, already in relationship with the Father, received the empowering of the Spirit in the context of prayer in order to preach the good news, and preached a message explaining the reality of his prophetic anointing (Lk. 3:21-22; 4:18-21). The disciples, already in relationship with Jesus, are about to receive an empowering of the Spirit which results in Peter's message explaining that empowering and preaching the good news (Ac. 2:5-39).

WHAT HAPPENED AT PENTECOST?

So far, this fits a pattern that Pentecostal teachers have set out. First we are saved, then we are empowered in our witness. But when we examine the work of the Spirit as Acts progresses, we notice that the Spirit is presented as far more than a simple external empowering to witness. The Holy Spirit gives wisdom (6:3, 5; 15:28), faith (11:24), direction (11:28) comfort (9:31) and joy (13:52) to believers. The Spirit sets leaders over the church (20:28). So what happened at Pentecost is not simply an empowering which comes subsequent to an initial conversion. Pentecost is presented as critical to the entire Christian life. Understanding Pentecost as a second, empowering experience does not seem to fit this perspective.

The disciples, unlike any who succeeded them, experienced the Spirit through Jesus' earthly ministry. But what happens when Jesus is taken up into heaven? The disciples could hardly live off their earthly memories of him. This explains the command of Jesus to wait in Jerusalem (Lk. 24:47-49; Ac. 1:18). There is only one power that can be given the disciples to continue the reality initiated in Jesus' earthly ministry, and that power is the Holy Spirit. That makes sense, as it was the power of the Spirit upon Jesus which initiated the breaking in of the kingdom in the first place. The outpouring of the Spirit will deepen the impact of the kingdom in and through the disciples, while at the same time enabling them to extend the kingdom further than they could ever have imagined while Jesus was with them.

So when Jesus gathered the disciples together before his ascension, he told them four things. *First*, they would be baptized with the Holy Spirit. *Second*, they would receive power when the Spirit was "poured out" or "came upon" them. This refers to the prophecy of Isa. 32:15-20 that the end-times "outpouring" of the Spirit would bring God's people into a new state of cleansing, peace and blessing. *Third*, they would be his witnesses. This alludes to the promise of Isa. 42:1-13 that in the last days Israel would be restored to be a witness to the nations. *Fourth*, they would go to the ends of the earth. This references Isaiah's promise of a Messianic figure who will not only restore Israel but will make her a light to the nations, "that my salvation may reach to the end of the earth" (Isa. 49:6).

This coming outpouring of the Spirit, therefore, involves a cleansing baptism of the Spirit and fire which will precipitate the beginnings of ancient prophetic promises concerning the restoration of God's people into a state of peace and prosperity, and who will bring this salvation of God to the very ends of the earth. All the promises God made to Israel are about to be fulfilled. So the outpouring of the Spirit is far more than just an empowering to witness. It will be the source of kingdom life and peace, and will enable a restoration of God's people so powerful their experience and life in God will overflow to the nations of the earth. *The Holy Spirit will be far more than a "charismatic anointing." He will be the source of a new life promised since Moses but never before realized.*

The promise of the Spirit is guaranteed to all who turn to the Lord, as Peter's message at Pentecost makes clear. After the Spirit falls at Pentecost, Peter explains to the astonished people what has happened. He quotes Joel 2:28-32 and states that what they are witnessing is the fulfilment of this prophecy (Ac. 2:17-21). After quoting several other Scriptures proving that Christ is the true successor of David, he urges them to repent and be baptized in water for the forgiveness of their sins, and they will receive the gift of the Holy Spirit (Ac. 2:38). This promise, which is for them and their children (Ac. 2:39), refers back to the prophecy of Joel that the Spirit would be poured out on their sons and daughters (see Ac 2:17). In fact, Peter continues, the promise is for "everyone" whom the Lord calls on God (Ac. 2:40, citing Joel 2:32). Therefore, the gift of the Spirit as poured out on Pentecost is for *every believer without exception.*

Peter's promise in Ac. 2:38 is normative for everyone who receives Christ *from the day of Pentecost onwards:* "Repent and be baptized every one of you in the name of Jesus Christ for the forgiveness of your sins, and you will receive the gift of the Holy Spirit." If this is the case, then the Spirit is from that moment on to be given to everyone who repents and witnesses to their repentance outwardly in baptism. This has a clear and unavoidable meaning: the baptism of the Holy Spirit refers to that event where a person repents, receives the Spirit and is baptized in water. *The baptism of the Holy Spirit, from a Biblical perspective, can only be understood to refer to a person's conversion, not to a theologically or spiritually separate subsequent event.* Contrary to Pentecostal teaching, the first disciples turn out to be a non-repeatable historical exception, in that their experience of Jesus began before Pentecost. This will never again apply to anyone else.

Therefore, we must reject the idea that Christians should seek an experience of the Holy Spirit as a form of blessing Biblically subsequent to their salvation. For the first disciples, the experience of salvation and the kingdom of God had already begun with Jesus' earthly ministry. Subsequent to that, they received power when the Holy Spirit came on them so that they could carry forward the ministry of Jesus. But from Pentecost onward, with Jesus now ascended to heaven, the gift of the Spirit was *the only way in which he was going to reveal himself on earth.* It would *henceforth* be impossible to encounter Jesus other than through the gift of his Spirit. There is nothing in the text of the first two chapters of Acts that indicates that Christians are supposed to recapitulate or repeat the experience of the first disciples. Their experience was unique and non-repeatable, in that it began in Jesus' earthly ministry and continued at Pentecost.

When Pentecost occurred, Peter realized that God had opened the doors of salvation to all those witnessing this amazing event. Salvation would come through repentance, followed by water baptism, and those who repented and were baptized would all *without exception* experience the gift of the Spirit. Thus repentance, water baptism and the gift of the Spirit are all linked as different but essential parts of the same event, which is the entrance of a person into the realm of God's salvation and his kingdom. The gift of the Spirit involved far more than a charismatic outward sign. The Spirit enabled the spread of the kingdom to the ends of the earth. The Spirit created and nurtured the kingdom life portrayed in the immediately following verses (Ac. 2:42-27), which encompassed worship, teaching, prayer and fellowship. To restrict discussion of the Holy Spirit to a dispute over tongues, no matter what position one takes on that subject, is to misunderstand the person and work of the Holy Spirit almost entirely.

THE TONGUES OF PENTECOST

We still have to address the assertion of Pentecostals and some charismatics that the receiving of the Spirit was always accompanied by tongues. The phenomenon of speaking in tongues was completely unknown in Judaism, and so marked something totally new. What happened to the disciples was actually a miraculously-given ability to speak in known foreign languages. This was not something experienced by Jesus at his baptism, when the empowering of the Spirit came upon him, nor does it seem to be mentioned again anywhere in Acts, or for that matter anywhere else in the New Testament. This seems to be connected with the idea that Pentecost is the undoing of Babel. Whereas God confused human language at Babel as part of the curse and the dispersing of the nations (Gen. 11:1-9), he undid the curse at Pentecost in order that the message of salvation might come to every nation. The comparison is reinforced by the use of the same verb in both passages. The miraculously-inspired multilingual prophetic praise of the disciples is a divine initiation of Jesus' promise that the gospel would go to every nation. This appears to differentiate the tongues at Pentecost from the miraculously-inspired speech elsewhere in Acts and Paul's letters, which Paul refers to as the "tongues of angels" (1 Cor. 13:2). These tongues required a separate gift of interpretation, as 1 Corinthians 12 and 14 indicates, whereas the tongues at Pentecost needed no interpretation.

WHAT HAPPENED AT SAMARIA?

If receiving the Spirit is part of the experience of conversion, then we might be puzzled by the events that unfolded at Samaria some time after Pentecost. Philip went to Samaria and preached the Gospel, accompanied by the performing of "signs and great miracles" (Ac. 8:13). The Samaritans, including one Simon, a magician, believed and were baptized. When the apostles heard the news, they went down to Samaria and "prayed for them that they might receive the Holy Spirit, for he had not yet fallen on any of them" (Ac. 8:15-16). As they laid their hands on the converts, they received the Spirit (verse 17), accompanied by some kind of visible phenomenon as witnessed by Simon, who then offered money to the apostles that he might receive the same gift (verse 19). This earned him a very stern rebuke from Peter (verses 19-23). In all this, no criticism is made of Philip's ministry. In fact, Philip is portrayed as a man "full of the Spirit" (Ac. 6:3-5) and a successful evangelist throughout the events recorded in Acts 8. Some suggest the Samaritans' faith was only in Philip and not Christ, but the statement is that they believed Philip *as he preached the kingdom and Christ* (verse 12), thus putting emphasis on the message rather than the one who delivered it. Simon himself appears to have been genuinely converted. What he was potentially excluded from was not the kingdom, but the ministry of the laying on of hands (verse 21). The fact that the apostles laid hands on the Samaritans rather than preaching to them and calling them to repentance suggests that they accepted their profession of faith as genuine. The description of what happened after the laying on of hands implies that something visible and extraordinary happened, such that it caught Simon's attention. The phrase "the Spirit had not yet fallen on any of them" is parallel to the description of the Spirit falling on Cornelius and the Gentiles (11:15). All this points to the fact that the laying on of hands occasioned a Samaritan Pentecost, in all probability with the evidence of prophecy or speaking in tongues (whether foreign or unknown). The Samaritans had only one receiving of the Spirit, and that was when the apostles arrived. It is safe to make the assumption that what caused the apostles to hasten to Samaria was that they heard that the Samaritans' expression of repentance accompanied by baptism was not also accompanied by a visible receiving of the Spirit, in line with the truth expressed by Peter in Ac. 2:38. The apostles themselves had known what it was to experience genuine faith long before the Spirit fell upon them. Hence, rather than being alarmed because the Samaritans were baptized before being converted, they accepted their faith as genuine but their overall experience as out of order with what had been revealed at Pentecost. There is little doubt that the Samaritan Pentecost was accompanied by a phenomenon similar to Pentecost, and we will have to consider what this may mean for the idea of tongues as an evidence of receiving the Spirit.

The arrival of the Gospel in Samaria marked the first step in the outward expansion of the kingdom beyond the Jews, in line with what Jesus had said, that the coming of the Spirit would cause them to be witnesses first in Jerusalem and Judea, then in Samaria, and finally to the "end of the earth" (Ac. 1:8). If there was a Jerusalem Pentecost, there might also be a Samaritan Pentecost. And if the carefully reconstituted full number of twelve apostles were to spearhead the government of God and extension of his kingdom, then those apostles, or the foremost among them, must be represented at each of these historical *but non-repeatable* Pentecosts. Did God allow a delay for this very reason? This may make better sense of the passage than interpreting it as endorsement of a distinct second blessing. The apostles did not endorse a second blessing, but rather were concerned *that the first experience of the converts was defective.*

CORNELIUS AND THE GENTILES

There is little doubt that Acts portrays the events at the house of Cornelius as the Gentile Pentecost. The gospel has come to the Jews and the Samaritans, now it extends (with Cornelius and his friends as representatives) to the "ends of the earth." If we had a Jerusalem Pentecost, followed by a Samaritan Pentecost, we now have a Gentile Pentecost. In both accounts, the "gift of the Holy Spirit" is "poured out" (10:45 = 2:17-18, 33). What happens to Cornelius and his friends is described as the fulfilment of the promise of John the Baptist concerning baptism in the Spirit (11:16), just as Jesus said to the disciples in 1:5. Both occasions involved a dramatic move of the Spirit accompanied by speaking in tongues. The Gentiles received the Spirit, just as the Jews did at Pentecost (10:47; 11:15-17). Peter's repeating of the account to the leaders at Jerusalem makes clear that the

Gentiles believed by hearing the "word of the gospel" (15:7), and that God then gave them "the Holy Spirit just as he did to us" (15:8), having "cleansed their hearts by faith" (15:9). This makes clear that their profession of faith in response to the gospel message was the initial key to their salvation, but the almost instantaneous reception of the Holy Spirit, as at Pentecost, shows that the receiving of the Spirit was an integral part of their entering the kingdom. This takes us back to Peter's declaration in Ac. 2:38 that repentance, baptism in the Spirit and baptism in water were all part of the same event of salvation. It was the receiving of the Spirit that allowed Peter to proceed with water baptism, as an outward sign of the Gentiles' incorporation into the people of true messianic Israel: "Then Peter declared, 'Can anyone withhold water for baptizing these people, who have received the Holy Spirit just as we have?' And he commanded them to be baptized in the name of Jesus Christ" (Ac. 10:47-48a). When Peter had to defend his actions in baptizing Gentiles to the Jerusalem Council, he said that God "bore witness to them, by giving them to Holy Spirit just as he did to us, and he made no distinction between them and us, having cleansed their hearts by faith" (Ac. 15:8-9). Hence he sees the gift of the Spirit and the cleansing by faith to be part of the same event. And this would make sense to Jews, who believed that the Spirit had been withdrawn because of Israel's sin, and would only be restored when the Messiah came to cleanse and renew Israel. If even the Gentiles were receiving the Spirit, they also must have experienced the Messiah's cleansing power.

And so the account of the conversion of the Gentiles makes clear that the Pentecostal gift of the Spirit is a non-negotiable and fundamental part of a believer's salvation. First the Spirit is outpoured at Pentecost, then in Samaria, and now on the Gentiles. In each case the three critical elements are present: repentance, receiving of the Spirit and water baptism.

THE DISCIPLES OF JOHN AT EPHESUS

One further account exists in Acts where the outpouring of the Spirit, accompanied by speaking in tongues, takes place. Paul returns to Ephesus after an initial brief visit described in Ac. 18:24-28, where he leaves Aquila and Priscilla as well as Apollos. With Apollos gone to Corinth, Paul finds a small group of "disciples" (Ac. 19:2). This group appears to have some knowledge of Jesus, but something in their response raises a question with Paul, who then inquires as to whether they received the Spirit when they believed. It turns out they have not even heard of the Holy Spirit, but know only the water baptism of John. Having realized that these men, though they may have heard of Christ, have not yet in fact been converted, he must explain to them the basic fact that John's ministry and baptism pointed to "the one who was to come after him, that is, Jesus" (verse 4). On hearing and responding to his gospel message, they received water baptism, during the process of which Paul laid hands on them, "the Holy Spirit came on them, and they began speaking in tongues and prophesying (verse 6). The "coming upon them" of the Spirit is just what Jesus referred to, using the same words, in 1:8, pointing to Pentecost. The signs that followed in this account expand the horizon of the Pentecostal gifts to include prophecy. Whatever the signs involved, it is clear throughout Acts that the receiving of the Spirit, where it is explicitly recorded, was a *visible phenomenon*.

IS THERE AN IDENTIFIABLE OUTWARD AND SUPERNATURAL EVIDENCE OF THE BAPTISM OF THE SPIRIT?

The immediate effect of the receiving of the Spirit was not only power to witness, but also seemed to involve for the first believers a life-long impartation of the Spirit enabling a faithful life and witness even until death. The argument on the subject of the outward evidence has long focussed on the occurrence of tongues at Pentecost and elsewhere in Acts, and whether what happened there is a template for what should happen all the time. Put another way, if the baptism of the Spirit was an observable phenomenon in these cases, what exactly does this mean? The Jewish reading of the Old Testament led to the conclusion that men like Samson, Saul, David, Elijah and others experienced dramatic manifestations when the Spirit came upon them, which then caused them to erupt in praise, prophecy or the working of miraculous deeds. The Spirit had been withdrawn from Israel due to the nation's sin, but they looked forward to the day the Spirit would return, and interpreted Joel's prophecy this way. They expected this to be fulfilled by men and women prophesying as the Spirit fell on them. The Jewish teachers also believed that the receiving of the Spirit served the purpose of validating those upon whom the Spirit came. The principal example of this in the Bible was when the Spirit came upon the seventy elders of Moses (Num. 11:10-30), thus validating their new role of leadership in the nation. The various prophetic manifestations of Luke 1 and 2 involving Elizabeth, Mary, Zechariah and Simeon would all qualify as the fulfilment of this kind of expectation, as did the ministry of John the Baptist and Jesus' experience of the Spirit coming upon him to preach in power and do signs and wonders. The Jewish people should have recognized such manifestations, taken together, to indicate the imminent arrival of the messianic age, which was why Jesus was puzzled that Nicodemus, as a prominent teacher, did not seem to understand the work of the Spirit.

Tongues, though something completely unknown to the Jews, would have been recognized as in line with these miraculous manifestations of the Spirit, which is why Pentecost had such a profound evangelistic impact. Jesus was left alone at the cross, and even after the resurrection the community of faith contained barely more than one hundred people, but at Pentecost thousands were immediately added.

Is tongues therefore the outward evidence of the baptism of the Spirit? The occasions in Acts where the falling of the Spirit was accompanied by tongues are all significant. They involved the three-stage breaking in of the kingdom spoken of by Jesus: at Pentecost to the Jews, at Samaria to the Samaritans and at the house of Cornelius to the Gentiles. The tongues in Jerusalem validated the Christian believers as true representatives of a new messianic age. The tongues at Samaria validated the previously racially-alienated converts of Samaria as part of true Israel. The tongues at the house of Cornelius opened the door of admission to true Israel even to the Gentiles. But does this mean that a similar experience is to be expected once those milestones have been reached? In other words, is there a need for Jewish converts after Pentecost to have their experience validated by tongues as outward evidence? Is there a need for Samaritan converts after Acts 8? Or a need for Gentile converts after Acts 10?

That is where the experience of the new converts at Ephesus might be helpful. Although they are not part of a new spiritually-significant people group receiving the Spirit for the first time, they do experience supernatural manifestations after Paul prays for them. According to 19:6, "they began speaking in tongues and prophesying." To proceed carefully, we note that this is a general description. If Luke had meant to say each had spoken in tongues, each had prophesied, or each had done both, he would have added the Greek adjective *hekastos* ("each") in the appropriate place instead of generalizing. What is reasonable to assume that that each of them probably experienced *some kind of manifestation*, whether it be tongues or prophecy. Prophecy, as defined by Jewish expectation, was defined broadly as a spontaneous outburst of praise and glory to God, not narrowly as words predicting future events. This is why the tongues of Pentecost, which are defined as "telling the mighty works of God," would have been regarded as a form of prophecy.

On the other hand, this is the only group of disciples of John the Baptist we encounter in Acts, and some scholars have thought that is why they had a supernatural Pentecostal experience: God was bringing to fulfilment for them the baptism of John. That would cause them to fall into another special and non-repeatable category as with the other three groups of people. This is possible, but not certain.

But it also has to be considered that significant conversions occur in Acts *without any mention of tongues or prophecy.* Think of the Ethiopian eunuch (8:38-39); of Paul (9:17-18, though he experienced a miracle of healing and later tells us he speaks in tongues [1 Cor. 14:18]); of Lydia (16:14-15); and of the Philippian jailer and his family (16:32-34). Signs and wonders of healing were done by the apostles

(5:12-16) and further conversions were numerous (4:4, 6:7), but without any further *explicit* mention of tongues accompanying these events.

What we have shown so far demonstrates that the falling of the Spirit upon people is the sign of their inclusion in the messianic covenant. Pentecost persuaded the Jews when Jesus' teaching had not. Old Testament prophecy, from Moses onward, pointed to the pouring out of the Spirit as a sign the latter-days reign of God's kingdom had arrived. Luke was not in the least interested in the modern debate over whether tongues is the sign of the outpouring of the Spirit, or whether in fact the charismata have ceased entirely, and so his primary concern is not to address such issues. What we can be sure of is that, when at critical points, the coming of the Spirit was accompanied by supernatural signs such as tongues and prophecy, it can hardly be the case that *when other early believers came to faith and received the Spirit, there were never any observable outward signs at all!* So the fact that such are not recorded in the case of every convert does not mean *nothing* happened. Conversion without any external manifestation of the Spirit would have left the apostles suspect that people had not received the Spirit at all, which was what happened at Samaria. If we add to this the evidence that the abundance of charismata at Corinth (if not their actual use) receives a ringing endorsement from Paul, it seems hardly likely that the apostolic churches were bereft of regular signs of the Spirit's presence, including certainly in conversion experiences.

Joel said that one sign of the Spirit coming would be that God's people would prophesy. According to Rev. 19:10, the "testimony of Jesus is the spirit of prophecy," meaning that those who testify to Jesus are by definition a prophetic people. When the Holy Spirit came on people at Pentecost, he enabled them to speak forth the praises of God. We should not get hung up about tongues. What we should insist on is that the Biblical norm is for every believer to receive the Spirit as a consequence of repentance for their sins, and that the pouring out of the Spirit upon that person will be manifest. What I mean by that is this. *When the Spirit comes, he takes us into a prophetic world,* a world in which we begin to experience the supernatural, a world in which God encounters us with the whole array of his supernatural gifts, a world in which God is more real than anything we can access with our five natural senses. *To leave the realm of the natural and enter the realm of the supernatural is at the heart of the gift of the Spirit and the difference he makes in our lives, and defines what it means to be a prophetic people.* A prophetic people are a people who have moved from darkness to light, a people who have encountered and entered the realm of the kingdom of God, a people whose lives have been once and for all definitively changed. If there is no sign at our conversion or following it that the Holy Spirit has impacted us in power and that our lives have been changed as a result, something is wrong. We may never speak in tongues, but we may encounter the Spirit in some other way. The gifts of the Spirit in the four lists Scripture gives us a range from prophecy to leadership. Our job is to be open to all he has to give us — how foolish not to be! For the empowerment of the Spirit is needed for God's people now more than ever in an age where our supernatural enemy will leave none of his weapons unused in his quest to destroy us.

HOW DO WE EXPLAIN THE FACT THAT MILLIONS HAVE RECEIVED WHAT APPEARS TO BE A SECOND BLESSING?

We must start by confessing that the church has often grieved the Holy Spirit by denying his gifts. The Holy Spirit appeared at Jesus' baptism as a dove (Matt. 3:16), a bird which will quickly fly off if trouble is sensed. Paul warns us: "Do not grieve the Holy Spirit of God" (Eph. 4:30). Over the centuries, the church grew cold and lost touch with the supernatural empowering of the Spirit. Teachers and theologians denied the church's need of the Spirit as received at Pentecost. We retained a doctrine of the Spirit but without his power. And thus we lost a vital part of true doctrine. So the Holy Spirit in measure withdrew, and we lost a very important dimension of who he is. Christians have even denied that God ever works supernaturally, even to heal the sick, saying that those miracles ceased after the days of the New Testament. Such teaching, which has no backing in the Bible (see the chapter on prophecy), is only a cover for our sinful rejection of God's power and our spiritual barrenness, which we have tried to justify instead of acknowledging and crying out for deliverance. The charismatic gifts have periodically emerged over the history of the church only to disappear again, but that changed with the outpouring of the Spirit at Azusa Street in the early 1900s, followed by the emergence of the charismatic movement in the 1960s, which has since spread across the globe to encompass hundreds of millions of believers. For the first time since the early centuries of its existence, the majority of the church worldwide would accept the present operation of the supernatural power of the Spirit. As people do reach out to God and begin to rediscover the fulness of the Holy Spirit's work, he has been busy restoring those realities in the church. Very often people have come to an encounter with the Holy Spirit, in which they have received what was supposed to be part of the original package when they first came to Christ. We could describe this as being re-filled with Spirit, along the lines of the prayer meeting in Acts 4 and what Paul teaches about the need to be continually re-filled in Eph. 5:18. Sad to say, it is possible to come to Christ, be born again and baptized in the Spirit without being truly filled with the Spirit in the way that the early church experienced and that God intended for every believer at salvation. This, however, is not God's Biblical ideal! And so let us avoid two mistakes. One is to deny that conversion involves a power encounter with the Holy Spirit because his gifts have long since ceased, and that conversion is merely an intellectual and non-verifiable or visible event. The other is to deny that conversion involves a power encounter with the Holy Spirit because *that can only be received* in a subsequent experience. If we teach either, we are guilty of grieving the Spirit.

PROPHECY

Peter's sermon in Acts 2 reflects the Old Testament expectation that the coming of the Messiah would be accompanied by the restoration of the Holy Spirit to God's people, and that this restoration would be marked above all by the fact that all God's people would prophesy (Ac. 2:17, quoting Joel 2:28).

What is prophecy? Is it the same in the New Testament as in the Old? How authoritative is it? What relationship does it have to the writing of Scripture? Does it exist today?

These questions are both contentious and very poorly understood by many believers. Prophecy is often understood as a series of predictions the Bible makes about the last days immediately before Jesus returns. Why this is wrong is examined in our chapter on eschatology. Very little Biblical prophecy is about predicting specific events in the days immediately prior to Christ's return. For others, prophecy is a weird phenomenon occurring in charismatic circles where people are caught up in a trance, and bring forth revelation they consider to be on the same level as the Bible. This portrayal of prophecy usually comes from people who have never actually encountered exercise of the prophetic gift, and is refuted by any who do have such experience. Yet undoubtedly there is a lot of chaff amidst the wheat. How do we separate it all out?

We need some answers. The best place to get them is the Bible itself. Let's take a quick survey of prophecy in the Old Testament and the New Testament. Then let's look at the differences and parallels. Finally, let's try to figure out what this means for us today.

PROPHECY IN THE OLD TESTAMENT

The Old Testament is full of prophetic ministry. Abraham is described as a prophet (Gen. 20:7). God designated Aaron as Moses' prophet (Exod. 7:1-2). Moses knew that he himself was a prophet, and said that one day God would raise up another prophet like him to lead Israel, a prophet the New Testament understands to be Christ (Deut.

18:15; Ac. 7:37). At his death, Moses was described as the greatest prophet, one with whom God spoke face to face, and who moved in miraculous signs and wonders (Deut. 34:10-12). The heart of Moses' ministry was leadership of the nation and keeping it faithful to the Lord, and his prophetic role must be seen in that light. But Moses had no monopoly on the prophetic ministry. In Num. 11:24-30, the Spirit came upon the elders of Israel and they prophesied. God gave directions to the Israelites to enable both true and false prophets to be identified. They were warned that even if a prophet's predictions are accurate, he must not be followed if he uses his supernatural gifting to lure people away from the Lord (Deut. 13:1-5). Prophets who honor the Lord must be listened to, but those who do not must be rejected (Deut. 18:14-22).

After Moses, the next great prophet was Samuel. Samuel was the only man other than Moses described as a prophet who brought leadership to Israel. Samuel moved in the supernatural prophetic gift, but the thrust of his ministry was devoted to bringing direction and justice to the nation. He was instrumental in establishing the kingship under Saul, and in passing on the kingship to David. In his day, there were roving bands of prophets whose ministry was accompanied by supernatural manifestations. When Saul came into contact with them, he also started prophesying (1 Sam. 10:1-8). Later, when Saul sent men to capture David, his men encountered a prophetic band led by Samuel and began to prophesy. When

Saul himself went, he came under the same prophetic spirit all day and all night (1 Sam. 19:19-24).

After the establishment of the kingship, the prophet's role became more focussed. He was to warn the king and the people when their actions were contrary to God's law, to call them to obey it, and to remind them of the consequences if they failed to do so. Under David's reign, the prophets Gad and Nathan played a role in keeping David faithful to the Lord (2 Sam. 12:1-14; 24:11-24). They were unafraid to intervene in matters of national significance, even when they were opposing the king. The next great prophets were Elijah and Elisha. By their time, kings were often unfaithful to the Lord. Elijah and Elisha both led prophetic groups (2 Kgs. 2:3; 4:1, 38; 6:1; 9:1). They moved in amazing supernatural signs and miracles of healing, but the heart of their ministry was to bring God's justice and direction to the nation, leading them into great conflict with reigning monarchs of Israel and Judah such as Ahab, Joram and Ahaziah.

After this came the time of the great writing prophets, those whose prophetic insights are recorded in books of Scripture under their own name. The majority of these prophets were active during three periods of national crisis, from the dying days of the northern kingdom (Amos, Hosea, Isaiah and Micah in the eighth century BC), through the decline of the southern kingdom (Jeremiah, Nahum, Zephaniah and Habakkuk in the seventh century

BC) to the time of the exile in Babylon (Ezekiel and Daniel in the sixth century BC). These were all prophets of the word; the miraculous (other than the visionary element) is secondary or not evident at all. Though they did predict future events, the heart of their ministry was to call the people to obedience to God, and to show them that what the future held depended on whether or not they were obedient to God's Word as revealed in his law. They warned repeatedly of coming judgment. But they also prophesied of God's salvation and merciful deliverance.

The ministry of the prophets was characterized by the fact they had a revelation of the ways of God, and a revelation of what would happen if those ways were not followed. Unlike a teacher of the law, who would expound the whole law in a balanced way, the prophet would focus narrowly, but with laser-like intensity, on particular areas where the law was being disobeyed, and would proclaim the consequences of this disobedience in the present and the future. The concept of prophetic revelation is expressed by the Hebrew word *chazah*, meaning "to see." As distinct from the verb which expresses ordinary physical vision, this word has a double meaning: either to see by understanding and perception into the ways and purposes of God, or to see by a supernatural vision. The prophets had an acute perception of God's word, and an ability to focus in on where it was being disobeyed. Without this revelation comes disaster. The prophets' revelation of the Word is expressed in their continuous confrontation of the kings and the people with specific acts of disobedience to God's law.

The prophets' revelation also took the form of supernatural visions concerning the future, either physical supernatural visions, as in the many visions of Daniel (e.g. 2:19, 45) or Ezekiel (e.g. chapters 1; 9-11; 40-48), or a mental vision in the sense of the revelation of future events (Hab. 2:2: "Write the vision; make it plain on tablets"). Whatever its nature, the vision or revelation is always based on the prophets' understanding of God's law, of the peoples' behavior toward it, and of the consequences of that behavior, whether positive or negative.

From beginning to end, the Old Testament prophets had as their greatest concern the establishment of righteousness and obedience to God's law in the nation. The prophets were not so much concerned with teaching the law as with challenging the rulers and the people with their deviations from it. They had the ability to focus on areas of rebellion, and the courage to declare the consequences of these. Through exhortation, revelation and vision, they warned of the disasters people would bring on themselves if they disobeyed God's law, but at the same time comforted them with the promise of future deliverance.

PROPHECY IN THE NEW TESTAMENT

In the New Testament, prophecy has two basic meanings. Sometimes, though not often, it refers to predicting the course of future events. Agabus prophesied the coming of a famine (Ac. 11:28). Judas and Silas prophesied many things which encouraged and strengthened the church at Antioch, though it is not recorded whether they made any predictions concerning the future (Ac. 15:32). Most often, however, it refers to bringing encouragement and strengthening to people to obey God's word in the situations they are in.

Paul tells us a few things about prophecy in 1 Corinthians 14. Prophecy is for strengthening, encouragement and comfort (14:3). Prophecy lays bare the secrets of peoples' hearts (14:25). Prophecy is not delivered in some religious trance but in a normal state of mind, where the person prophesying can stop and start at will, is sensitive to revelation being given to others and will courteously step aside to give others an opportunity (14:29-32). A variety of prophetic gifts will operate. Potentially, any member of the Body can move in the gift of prophecy: "For you can all prophesy one by one" (1 Cor. 14:31). However, only two or three people should prophesy in any given meeting, and the rest of the congregation should weigh or evaluate these prophetic words: "Let two or three prophets speak, and let the others weigh what is said" (1 Cor. 14:29). The word for "others" here refers to the congregation as a whole (not just "other prophets"), which therefore has the responsibility of weighing the word given in light of Scripture.

The verb to "comfort" or "encourage" (*parakalein*) is key to our understanding of New Testament prophecy. It is used in connection with prophecy in Ac. 15:32, where the prophets Judas and Silas "encouraged" the brothers. Paul gives the purpose of prophecy twice in one chapter: "The one who prophesies speaks to people for their upbuilding and encouragement and consolation" (1 Cor. 14:3). And again in 14:31: "For you can all prophesy one by one, so that all may learn and all be encouraged."

This basic function of encouragement traces back to the role of the Holy Spirit. Preparing them for his departure, Jesus told his disciples: "And I will ask the Father, and he will give you another Helper [*parakletos*], to be with you forever, even the Spirit of truth" (Jn. 14:16-17). The Greek word *parakletos* is the noun form of the same verb "to comfort/encourage." It refers to a legal representative or advocate who comes forward to defend and help those in trial. The function of New Testament prophecy is to bring encouragement from God to those in the heat of battle to stay faithful and keep persevering until victory comes. That is one of the main purposes of the book of Revelation.

In 1 Cor. 12:28, Paul states that God has appointed first apostles, second prophets, third teachers and then various others. The existence of prophets is clear from the earliest days of the church. A group of prophets, including Agabus (who appears again in Ac. 21:10), came down from Jerusalem to minister in the church at Antioch (Ac. 11:27-28). A team of prophets and teachers existed in that same church (Ac. 13:1). It is interesting that Paul and Barnabas, who later went on to apostolic ministry, are listed in this group, showing that apostles could function prophetically. Judas and Silas (also later named as an apostle), leaders in the Jerusalem church, went down to Antioch with Paul and Barnabas to deliver the decisions reached at the council of Jerusalem. They are described as prophets who brought strength and encouragement to the church (Ac. 15:22-35).

There are three functions of New Testament prophecy:

To comfort, upbuild and strengthen. In many passages dealing with prophecy, "encourage" means to bring comfort and strength in the face of the difficulties and struggles of life. In 1 Cor. 14:3, "encouragement" appears alongside "upbuilding" and "consolation." In Ac. 15:32, "encourage" appears together with "strengthen." In other passages where the idea of encouragement or comfort appears, though not in a context relating to prophecy, it is accompanied by references to God's sustaining promise, which strengthens us against temptation (Heb. 6:18), the encouragement or comfort of the Scriptures which gives us hope (Rom. 15:4), the love, hope and strengthening which comes from both the Father and the Son (2 Thess. 2:16-17), or the encouragement Paul experiences through receiving good news (1 Thess. 3:7; 2 Cor. 7:6,13). Prophecy is meant to bring comfort, strengthening and a message of hope for those in distress. Prophecy reassures people that God is still with them, and does so in a way that, under the anointing of the Spirit, has a great impact. This may occur through the person prophesying having supernatural insight into the lives of others.

To exhort and challenge. Encouragement consists not only of bringing comfort, but also entails a challenge to walk closer to the Lord. Prophecy exhorts people toward a deeper level of obedience. In 1 Cor. 14:31, the prophetic ministry both encourages and teaches. This does not involve condemnation, but consists of exhortation that, by the power of the Spirit, each of us can walk in obedience to the Lord. In 1 Cor. 14:24, the prophet brings conviction of sin along with the encouragement and strengthening mentioned in verse 3 of that chapter, such that an unbeliever entering a room where a prophet is operating will, through the prophet's supernatural revelation, have the secrets of his heart laid bare and fall down in repentance and worship.

To reveal mysteries and knowledge. Paul wrote the following: "And if I have prophetic powers, and understand all mysteries and all knowledge..." (1 Cor. 13:2). What does this mean? Prophecy deals with the hidden mysteries and knowledge (or purposes) of God which are inaccessible to natural reason. God has clearly revealed his will in Scripture, but often the *application* of that to our present circumstances is not self-evident. New Testament prophecy does not add to Scripture, but can bring insight into the strategies of God. This may come, as it did with Daniel, through the interpretation of dreams (Ac. 27:23 might be an example). Or it might come through a vision, like the one Paul describes in 2 Cor. 12:1-10, which unveiled the purpose of God for his sufferings, or the one he describes in Ac. 16:9 which led him to pursue a course of action other than what the natural circumstances suggested. Or it could come through prayer. Have you ever suddenly realized while praying what the answer to your problem is? That could be a prophetic insight.

WHAT IS THE DIFFERENCE BETWEEN OLD TESTAMENT AND NEW TESTAMENT PROPHECY?

Greater level of authority. The main distinction between Old Testament and New Testament prophecy concerns the vastly different measures of authority. Understanding this is of critical importance to determining the question of whether prophecy is still in any sense valid today.

The Old Testament prophets were national prophets who reminded Israel of the blessings attached to obedience to the law, and the curses that would come if they disobeyed. The Old Testament prophets had authority to pronounce judgments on disobedience which would cut people off from God and from his people. Many, though by no means all, Old Testament prophecies were, under divine inspiration, written down and recorded as part of Scripture. As such, they remain authoritative for us today. They illustrate the consequences of certain patterns of sin and disobedience which still speak to us. They show how God's great plan of salvation was fulfilled in Christ, which adds to our understanding of who Christ is and what he has done for us.

New Testament prophecy operates under grace, and with the message of salvation through Christ. New Testament prophecy speaks to individuals and churches rather than to nations. Prophecy occasionally predicts future events such as a coming famine (Ac. 11:27-30) and Paul's arrest in Jerusalem (Ac.21:10-11), but such instances are rare. New Testament prophecy is not written down and incorporated into Scripture. It does not carry the authority prophecy did in the Old Testament.

Let's look at two apparent exceptions. First, what about John the Baptist? John the Baptist is a transitional figure between Old and New Testament prophecy. Jesus said: "There has arisen no one greater than John the Baptist," but added: "Yet the one who is least in the kingdom of heaven is greater than he" (Mt. 11:11). John was in one sense the last of the Old Testament prophets, preaching a message of repentance and judgment. He carried the authority of the forerunner of the Messiah. In that sense, John's ministry is not representative of New Testament prophecy. But what about Revelation? In this case, the exception proves the rule. John regarded himself as a prophet in the line of the Old Testament prophets and claimed their authority. He introduced his divine commissioning ("I was in the Spirit," Rev. 1:10) by using language similar to Ezekiel's (2:2, 3:12, 14, 24). Thus he places himself on a level with the Old Testament prophets. This is reinforced by his hearing of a "loud voice like a trumpet" similar to that heard by Moses in Exod. 19:16-20. This is why the prophecy given to John known to us as the book of Revelation is handed down to us as part of the New Testament canon, just like the writings of the Old Testament prophets. The New Testament does not contain anything similar to Revelation in terms of prophetic content. The prophetic ministry in the New Testament was for the moment in which it was given, and hardly any of it survives as direction for us today. We know that prophecy occurred, but the content is neither relevant nor authoritative for us, and hence, apart from fragments of prophetic words given for specific and non-repeatable occasions (the famine in Judea in Ac. 11:27-30; the warning to Paul in Ac. 21:11), it is not preserved as part of Scripture.

Distinctive possession of the Spirit. This vast difference in the levels of authority is related directly to the fact that in the Old Testament, the prophets had a unique anointing of the Spirit. Outside of the prophets and the godly kings, only a very few unrelated individuals such as Balaam, Bezalel and judges such as Gideon, Samson and Othniel are mentioned as in some sense experiencing the Holy Spirit. Even these are probably included because they functioned prophetically. As Christians, we take the Spirit's indwelling of believers as a well-established fact, but we have to remember that under the old covenant this was not the case. This set apart those who did experience the Spirit as people with unusual authority of some sort. This authority was often expressed in their prophetic writing becoming part of the Scriptures because God was speaking directly through them. The Jewish teachers believed the Spirit had departed entirely with the death of the last of the prophets. And so what happened at Pentecost, with its fulfillment of Joel's prophecy regarding the outpouring of the Spirit on all flesh, was so earth-shaking that thousands who had rejected Jesus in his earthly ministry were that day swept into the kingdom. But the initiation of a covenant in which all believers, not just one or two in each generation, were filled with the Spirit, had radical implications. Now all, potentially, could function prophetically, as Joel had said would be the case. That means necessarily that the authority of such prophetic utterances is drastically reduced.

Anointing to write Scripture. Much of the Old Testament contains the writings of the prophets. This is no longer true in the New Testament. The writing of Scripture, with the exception of Revelation, *becomes more of an apostolic than prophetic function.* Many scholars argue that apostles are the successors of the Old Testament prophets. Even John wrote his Gospel as an apostle, not just as a prophet. It is true that some New Testament writers were not apostles. Yet these exceptions carry less weight than we might think. For instance, Mark's Gospel receives authority from his close connection to Peter, and Luke the same from his connection to Paul. James was the brother of Jesus and a prominent leader in the early church.

Points of continuity. In spite of all this, there are similarities between the prophets of the two covenants. We would expect this to be the case, or else New Testament prophets would be called something completely different. The prophet's role is still to bring comfort, much as Isaiah did (40:1-2; 41:8-16; 42:1-9). He also still brings an exhortation to obedience, again also like Isaiah (1:16-20; 45:22-25; 50:10; 51:1-8). The prophet is still concerned about the presence of righteous behaviour among the people of God. The prophet still operates in supernaturally-given revelation. He still has a sense of the direction and purpose of God. He still holds high the standard or ideal God calls us all toward. He is still involved in charting the course and direction of God's people on earth. Prophetic ministry seems to have played a significant role in the New Testament church.

PROPHETS AND PROPHECY TODAY

Two main arguments are made that prophecy cannot exist today.

1. Continuing prophecy would mean adding to the Bible. One of the main objections levelled against the existence of prophetic ministry after the apostolic age is the connection of prophecy with the writing of Scripture. If prophecy continues, the argument goes, then the Bible must be considered open-ended. What is to prevent a contemporary prophecy from being given a status equal in authority to Scripture? This is based on the fact that Old Testament prophets frequently had their writings recorded as Scripture.

The first point to make is that being an Old Testament prophet and writing Scripture are by no means one and the same. Not everything Isaiah, Jeremiah, Ezekiel or others wrote became part of the Bible. What we have is almost certainly only a small part of what they spoke or wrote over their lifetime. So their status as prophets did not automatically give everything they said a place in Scripture. Most prophets never made it to this level at all. Think of some of the greatest prophets like Elijah and Elisha. A few of their actions and prophetic words were recorded, but only as part of the historical narrative. One can presume that even these were only a very small fraction of their life's work. Elisha is estimated to have prophesied for sixty years! Some, like Micaiah son of Imlah in 1 Kings 22, or the man of God who came from Judah to prophesy against Jeroboam at Bethel in 1 Kings 13, make cameo appearances. There were many unnamed and unknown prophets like those in Elisha's prophetic school (2 Kings 2). So even under the old covenant, not all prophets and prophesies were equal. *Just because you were a prophet did not mean what you spoke or wrote would become part of the Bible.*

What can be said is that the level of authority given to prophecy in the old covenant made it possible for some of the prophets to have some of their writings recorded as Scripture. The Old Testament prophets are presented, however, as speaking the word of God, and this was not to be questioned. That is why such a severe test was applied to them. If their prophecies did not come true, they were to be put to death (Deut. 18:22).

When we come to the New Testament, however, the writing of Scripture is connected with the apostles, not prophets. New Testament prophecy is much more limited in authority. According to 1 Cor. 14:29, it is to be weighed by the congregation as a whole. Can you imagine a committee of Israelites gathered to weigh the prophecies of Elijah or Jeremiah? Either you obeyed God and accepted them, or you disobeyed God and rejected them. You didn't have the option of weighing them in a congregational meeting!

So the argument that prophecy cannot exist today because it would necessarily mean adding to Scripture is invalid.

2. The gifts of the Spirit, including prophecy, ceased with the closing of the apostolic age. This doctrine is known as cessationism. It argues that the gifts of the Spirit ceased with the closing of the New Testament canon, and hence prophecy no longer exists. Biblical proof is claimed to be found in 1 Cor. 13:8, where is it stated that prophecy, tongues and knowledge will pass away "when the perfect comes." It is argued that the partial knowledge of the Corinthians is being contrasted with the complete knowledge that will come when the New Testament has been completed. But how could the Corinthians have possibly interpreted "the perfect" as the closing of the canon of Scripture when such a meaning of perfection is neither in the context nor anywhere else in the Bible? Further, in verse 12 Paul defines the coming state of perfection as one in which we will know God in the same way he knows us. Could it be said of the second century church that they even knew God better than the apostolic church, let alone knew him perfectly? He adds in verse 12 that when perfection comes, we will see the Lord face to face. Clearly he is speaking of the return of the Lord.

It is further argued that miracles were needed as supernatural testimony to the power of the Gospel during the years of the early church, but that when the New Testament was completed, the Bible itself is the only testimony now needed. But the presence of miracles constituted a sign that in Jesus the new age had arrived and the kingdom had broken in. Isa. 42:1-9 had prophesied that the miraculous would characterize the messianic age, and when Jesus began to open the eyes of the blind, Isaiah's words had come to pass. The messianic age lasts longer than the first century church! The outpouring of the Spirit at Pentecost *and the accompanying supernatural manifestations* are identified by Peter as the sign that the prophesied last days have arrived. These continuing demonstrations of the presence of the Spirit among believers, along with the accompanying signs, are therefore to characterize the last days. The New Testament consistently defines the last days as the period commencing with Pentecost and ending with the Lord's return. If this seems strange to us, consider these comments also made in our chapter on eschatology. In Ac. 2:17-21, Peter declares that at Pentecost the "last days" prophesied by Joel have begun, and he moves immediately and seamlessly in interpreting Joel as announcing both Pentecost (verses 17-19), and (without apparent time delay) the prophesied day of the Lord (the last judgment) in verses 19-21. Thus he collapses all of history after Christ into the category of the last days, and declares we are living in them now. A similar understanding of the last days is found in Hebrews ("In these last days he has spoken to us by his Son," 1:2), James ("You have laid up treasure in the last days," 5:3), and Peter ("[He] was made manifest revealed in the last times," 1 Pet.1:20). John interprets it this way himself, "Children, it is the last hour" (1 Jn. 2:18). The last days, spanning the period of time from Christ's death to his return, is to be characterized *from beginning to end* by the performing of miracles which attest and accompany the preaching of the kingdom.

IF PROPHECY IS FOR TODAY, HOW DO WE HANDLE IT?

If the existence of prophecy today makes us uncomfortable, it may help us to ask a basic question: do we believe God still speaks to us? We would all agree that he does. He speaks to us through our personal reading of the Bible, through preaching, through prayer, through the wise counsel of others and even through circumstances. Occasionally, people even have dreams they would consider significant. Why can he not speak through prophecy? Rev. 19:10 says that "the testimony of Jesus is the spirit of prophecy." Those who testify to Jesus are all those who believe in him. And all these people have a prophetic spirit. The statement thus means that we are a prophetic people, a people who by various means can still hear from God.

We need to demystify prophecy. Prophecy in one sense is simply an inspired application of Biblical truth. It often includes a dimension which requires supernatural information about people or circumstances. We have all heard of people awoken in the middle of the night to pray for someone, and it then turns out that person was in danger at that very hour. That is a prophetic prayer. When we bring counsel to someone that involves specific circumstances in their lives we could not know about, that is prophetic counsel, even if we do not think of it as such. Have we ever brought wisdom to someone, who then said, "How did you know I was struggling with that?" That is prophetic wisdom. Most of us have been prophesying without even knowing it!

New Testament prophecy does not carry the weight of the Old Testament prophets. The fact that it is to be weighed (1 Cor. 14:29) shows that it cannot be given as an oracle from God. Prophecies should be delivered in humility, rather than the person presuming to be a pipeline from God. It is not necessary or helpful to reinforce prophecy by prefacing it with the words "Thus says the Lord," as if that implies that the voice of God is coming directly through you and must not be questioned. Prophecy should always be given with a "way out." It should never be presented in black and white terms which leave the recipient feeling either they must accept it or they are in disobedience to God. It is often wise instead to preface a prophetic word with: "I believe/feel God is/may be saying," to indicate a posture of humility and a willingness to be corrected.

New Testament prophecy is always "in part." That is why Paul insisted on a variety of people prophesying. No prophecy captures the whole picture or the whole truth. That's why prophecy is clearly distinguished from the time when we will know everything (1 Cor. 13:9-12). No prophecy should present itself as the complete answer to someone's circumstances.

Prophecy is to be carefully evaluated before it is accepted. The wheat should be accepted and the chaff discarded, but the prophet is not to be stoned! However, greater weight will (rightly) end up being given to prophetic words from someone with an established track record of being correct.

I have had countless wonderful experiences with prophecy, both on the giving and the receiving end. A young man approached me in one city and asked how he could discern whether he was hearing something from God. As I was about to give counsel, I felt the Lord wanted to speak through me this one word, "Surrender!" And to say this in spite of the fact it did not seem a valid answer to his question. He immediately collapsed, sobbing. A week before God had spoken to him to surrender his life to Christ. He had asked for a sign, and the sign was this, that God would send him a man who would speak the one word "surrender" to him. On another occasion, I told a young man God would use his gift as a videographer to give him influence in the highest places of political power in a nation. Months later, he was working for a man who subsequently became the Prime Minister of the nation. I had a prophetic vision over a couple where they would encounter lightning rods and be used nationally in childrens' ministry. Six years later they bought a farm with house and barn covered in lightning rods. They got involved in homeschooling, and at time of writing are distributing a national home school curriculum across the United States. Many times my wife and I have spoken prophetic words over couples unable to have children who subsequently conceived, most against all medical odds.

Prophecy, just as Paul said, deals with mysteries and knowledge (1 Cor. 13:2). Prophecy shows us how God is at work in situations otherwise impossible for us to understand. Prophecy gives people and churches a sense of direction from God above and beyond what can be discerned from natural circumstances. Prophecy shows us to how to work together with God in the execution of his purposes. Many times believers find themselves working against God, for lack of knowledge as to what God is doing in a situation. We rebuke the devil for something God is actually doing, especially in times of testing and hardship. Prophecy brings a divinely-revealed wisdom which gives us a sense of direction. It does not replace the Bible, nor even come close to doing so. But it does take Biblical truth and help us to apply it in our lives. We live in an age where it seems the devil is speaking all over the place. Surely God is able to communicate with his people, and surely we need to hear him!

THE KINGDOM
OF GOD

The great theologian Abraham Kuyper made this statement: "There is not one square inch of this earth over which Christ does not cry, "Mine!" Kuyper put his words into effect. He founded a major Christian university, a Christian political party, and eventually became Prime Minister of the Netherlands. Kuyper's declaration was about the advancing of the kingdom of God. But do we really understand what that kingdom is?

THE KINGDOM MANDATE

The kingdom of God, put very simply, is the reign of God. All we usually see in the story of the Garden is our fall and ejection from God's presence. But that fails to understand its full significance. From the beginning of the Bible, God's intention was to establish his reign on the earth. Eden, where God had established his earthly rule and where he had placed his presence, was his temple. But it covered only a small portion of that creation. Then in Gen. 1:28, God gave Adam and Eve a further commission: "And God said to them, 'Be fruitful and multiply and fill the whole earth and subdue it…'" The means by which this goal was to be accomplished is stated in verse 27: "So God created man in his own image, in the image of God he created him; male and female he created them." Because they were created in his image, they were able to reflect and to enforce his rule over the whole earth. In other words, Adam and Eve were God's vice-rulers or vice-regents on earth. Not only were they to serve and guard within the Garden-temple, they were to extend its boundaries outward into the hostile and alien lands outside — the lands into which they were eventually expelled. God's goal was that the whole creation would be made habitable for Adam and his descendants, and that through them his rule would extend over it. This is confirmed by Isa. 45:18: "For thus says the Lord, who created the heavens… who formed the earth and made it (he established it; he did not create it empty, he formed it to be inhabited!)…" The ultimate goal of God was that, through the earth being subdued and made habitable, he himself would be glorified throughout his creation. The presence of God, which was initially limited to the Garden- temple of Eden, was to be extended throughout the whole world by his image-bearers.

THE ADVANCE OF THE KINGDOM IS STALLED

As the Bible makes clear, however, Adam failed in his task. He did not guard the Garden-temple, but permitted the entrance of the evil serpent who brought sin and rebellion into the very place of God's presence. Instead of extending the divine presence outward, Adam and Eve were cut off from that presence. But God, in his great mercy, had not given up on his creation, for Adam's commission was passed on to others. This explains why God commanded Noah to be fruitful and multiply and fill the earth (Gen. 9:1, 7). It explains why God promised Abraham that he would multiply his descendants and make him fruitful (Gen. 17:2, 6, 8), and why he said that in Abraham's seed all the nations of the earth would be blessed (Gen. 22:17-18). It explains why God told Isaac he would multiply his descendants and that all the nations of the earth would be blessed by them (Gen. 26:4). It explains why God told Jacob to be fruitful and multiply, and that a company of nations would come from him (Gen. 35:11-12). And it explains why it is recorded of Israel that they lived in Egypt and were fruitful and became very numerous (Gen. 47:27). And finally, it is also why on the eve of their entry into the promised land, God told Israel he would bless them, multiply them, make them fruitful and enable them to fill the earth by subduing the nations around them (Deut. 7:13-16).

And notice another interesting phenomenon. Every time, from Noah to Jacob, that God spoke these words of command and promise, renewing the commission to Adam, these men responded by (1) pitching a tabernacle (2) on a mountain, (3) building an altar, (4) worshiping God, and (5) almost always calling the place the house of God. The combination of these five elements occurs elsewhere in the Old Testament only in the the building of the tabernacle of Moses and the temple of Solomon. What is happening? The patriarchs are building worship areas in fulfillment of the original commission of Gen.1:26-28 that their offspring are to spread out to extend God's kingdom by subduing the world from the base of a divine temple.

THE SIGNIFICANCE OF THE TABERNACLE

The tabernacle was in fact a miniature form of the Garden. Adam and Eve had been given a task in the Garden — to work it and keep it. The same two Hebrew words are used of the work of the priests in the tabernacle and temple. The Garden was actually a temple, with Adam and Eve as its priests. This explains why in the tabernacle and temple there were cherubim who guarded the ark, why there were gourds, trees and pomegranates carved into the walls, why the main gate was on the east as in the garden and why there was a seven-branched candelabra, representing the tree of life. The tabernacle was a replication of the Garden-temple, though in miniature form and with severely restricted access.

And there is something even more fascinating. God deliberately designed the whole camp, centering upon the tabernacle, according to the pattern of Egyptian military encampments of that time. Egyptian camps had the same three-part form to the sacred structure that stood at the centre, the identical measurements, the same orientation toward the east, and were similarly surrounded by troops divided into four units. In the innermost room of the central three-chambered structure there was an idol of Pharaoh, which rested with two winged creatures on either side. The Egyptians believed that the soul of Pharaoh resided in the idol, so that Pharaoh was with them, whether he was physically present or not. What was the point God was making? He was sending a message to the Egyptians, as well as giving a revelation to his people Israel of who he was and what he was going to do for them. Even as the idolatrous Pharaoh led his troops from the innermost chamber, so the God of Israel was leading his troops from the Most Holy place, where it was no idol but his majestic presence which rested. *Israel's tabernacle was a travelling war headquarters from which God, in his place of rest, directed his troops until they achieved total victory.*

A NEW EDEN IS COMING

Israel, like Adam, failed to fulfill the commission. The priests of God's temple, as early as the days of Eli and as late as the days of Annas and Caiaphas, became corrupt and allowed evil into its innermost parts. Yet centuries later, with the nation destroyed and in exile, Ezekiel was still prophesying that God's original commission to Adam would one day be fulfilled: "And I will give you a new heart... and I will put my Spirit within you... You shall dwell in the land I gave to your fathers... I will cause the cities to be inhabited... And they will say, 'This land that was desolate has become like the garden of Eden...' then the nations that are left around you shall know that I am the Lord" (Ezek. 36:26-28, 33-36). Ezekiel is prophesying that God's people would go forth and fill the earth, extend the kingdom and begin to restore the Garden-temple! The end-time Eden that Ezekiel prophesies is then identified in chapters 40-48 as a temple, depicted symbolically in terms borrowed from the description of the Garden. This temple is not like former temples, but will extend over all of God's people living in the prophesied new promised land which is initiated in the church but comes to its fulfilment in the eternal city of Revelation 21-22.

In this latter-day temple, God's presence would be over all his people and would no longer be restricted to a physical place containing an ark. Isaiah says the same thing:"For the Lord comforts Zion; he comforts all her waste places and makes her wilderness like Eden, her desert like the garden of the Lord" (Isa. 51:2-3). This ever-expanding restored Garden- temple is prophesied again several chapters later: "Enlarge the place of your tent... do not hold back; lengthen your cords and strengthen your stakes. For you will spread abroad to the right and to the left, and your offspring will possess the nations" (Isa. 54:2-3). Then Isaiah strains forward to see something we do not meet again until John's vision of the Garden-temple of Revelation 21: "O afflicted one, storm-tossed and not comforted, behold, I will set your stones in antimony, and lay your foundations with sapphires. I will make your pinnacles of jasper and your gates of crystal, and all your walls of precious stones" (Isa. 54:11-12).

THE COMMISSION FULFILLED IN JESUS

Matthew's Gospel begins with the Greek expression *biblos geneseos*, literally, the "book of the beginning" or the "book of genesis." The only other places in the Greek Bible this phrase occurs are in Gen. 2:4, which reads literally: "This is the book of the genesis of the heavens and the earth," and Gen. 5:1 (again reading literally): "This is the book of the genesis of Adam." Matthew uses the phrase to make two things clear, first that he is narrating the record of a new genesis, a new creation in Christ, and second that Jesus is the last Adam. Whereas Israel spent forty years in the wilderness succumbing to the devil, Jesus spent forty days in the desert overcoming him, accomplishing the defeat of the devil that should have occurred in the Garden. After his defeat of Satan, Jesus begins to reconstitute the true Israel by appointing twelve apostles who, representing the church composed of Jew and Gentile alike, replace the twelve tribes of Israel as the government of God in the new covenant. His healings and miracles represent the beginning of the restoration of creation from its fallen state, and the fulfilment of what Isaiah prophesied when Israel would undergo her end-time restoration to God: "Then the eyes of the blind shall be opened, and the ears of the deaf unstopped; then shall the lame man leap like a deer, and the tongue of the mute sing for joy" (Isa. 35:5-6).

JESUS AND THE KINGDOM

Daniel had an extraordinary vision, one in which he saw a stone striking the idolatrous statue representing the kingdoms of the earth, and becoming a great mountain which fills the whole earth (Dan. 2:34-35). This mountain-temple is the same thing as "the mountain of the house of the Lord" (Isa. 2:2-3), the holy hill or mountain referred to throughout the Old Testament (Jer. 26:18; Mic. 4:1; Ps. 15:1, 43:3; Isa. 66:20). It is Mount Zion, which is God's temple, the place of his presence.

Quoting Psalm 118:22, Jesus presented himself as the cornerstone of a new temple (Mt. 21:42). Two verses later, he made the statement: "And the one who falls on this stone will be broken to pieces; and when it falls on anyone, it will crush him." (Mt. 21:44). This is a direct reference to Daniel's prophecy of the stone which would strike the idolatrous kingdoms and itself become a kingdom-temple that would never be destroyed. God's kingdom, present now in Jesus himself, would eventually crush everything that opposes it.

At the moment of his ascension, having subdued all his foes, he entered his rest, as surely as God the Father had done at creation. And when he ascended and sat down at the right hand of God, he began his rule, just as God the Father had done in the garden, at the tabernacle and in the temple. That is why it was at the moment before his ascension that Jesus said: "All authority in heaven and on earth has been given to me. Go therefore and make disciples of all nations... And behold, I am with you always, to the end of the age" (Mt. 28:18). So when Jesus gave his disciples the great commission to take the kingdom to the ends of the earth, *he was renewing the commission of Genesis and declaring its fulfilment in him.* Jesus would not fail.

We who are Christians are the temple of God. And as God's presence expands to fill his worldwide temple, God's people are commissioned with worldwide authority. God's people are meant to exercise God's authority on earth. We are a "holy temple in the Lord," of which Christ Jesus is the "cornerstone" (Eph. 2:20-21). In him we are "being built together for a dwelling place for God by the Spirit" (Eph. 2:22). God is now resting in this new temple in a way far more powerful than he ever rested in the old temple or the tabernacle. Not only that, this is a world-wide temple. Wherever Christians are, there is the dwelling place of God. The kingdom of God is being extended all over the world in a way Moses and Solomon could never have dreamed of. God calls us to enter his rest with him: "For we who have believed enter that rest" (Heb. 4:3). Faith is what motivated the long list of heroes in Hebrews 11, what drove them, what made them great. Faith takes our inheritance in the unseen realm and makes it flesh and blood reality in this world. The Israelites failed to enter God's rest and fulfill God's commission because they refused to believe the Word of God, but faith does not need any proof other than what God has said. The Word of God is the only evidence faith requires. Faith is the title deed to our inheritance. Let's wave our title deed in the devil's face and start taking possession of what God has given to us by his Spirit, at the inestimable cost of the blood of Christ.

"All authority in heaven and on earth has been given to me," Jesus said as he began to give his great commission. But his next words catch us up in this mission: "Go therefore and make disciples of all nations." How do you connect possessing the authority with completing the mission? In one word: faith. By faith we strive. By faith we make every effort to take hold of the promise that Jesus has that authority and we can confidently move out on the basis of it, even to the risking of our lives. Dr. David Livingstone, the great missionary to Africa, whose life work can be credited today with tens of millions of believers, was found dead in the jungle on his knees with his Bible opened at these final verses of Matthew 28, with the very last verse underlined: "And behold, I am with you always, to the end of the age." And in that very instant David Livingstone, a man who had given up everything for the call of God, walked into that heavenly celebration, had his name called out by the angels, was ushered into the very presence of God, took his place of rulership alongside his Lord and Savior, and entered into the fulfillment of his eternal rest. He had begun the work of extending the temple of God into a whole continent.

The Bible ends as it began. Its last two chapters fulfil its first two chapters. The river is there, and so are the precious stones. The tree of life is there, and so is the presence of God. The garden temple is restored, and the only difference is that the serpent is cast out.

Our task is to take the kingdom to the ends of the earth before Christ returns. This fulfils Jesus' words: "And this gospel of the kingdom will be proclaimed throughout the whole world as a testimony to all nations, and then the end will come" (Matt. 24:14).

THE KINGDOM AND THE CHURCH

There is only one problem. God has chosen a specific way to extend his kingdom, and it's a way many have walked away from. A long time ago, a Catholic theologian disillusioned with the institutional church made the statement: "Jesus preached the kingdom, but got the church." Sometimes we feel the same way. The kingdom is a wonderful thing — it's too bad we have to put up with the church. We become disillusioned with the human dimension of Christianity, even though we ourselves are part of the problem. Yet the church in all its weakness is still God's only instrument to reach men and women for Jesus Christ.

The problem with our experience of church comes when church is divorced from the power of the kingdom, and all we are left with is imperfect people. And then disappointment sets in, disappointment with God and with his people. And that's a killer. It's a very real phenomenon across our rationalistically-indoctrinated and materially-obsessed western world. We cannot fulfill our mandate to extend the kingdom to the ends of the earth unless we embrace the fact God has chosen the church, with all its imperfections, to do it. But the church needs to rediscover the power of the kingdom, or it risks losing massive numbers of people who find it lacking in the raw spiritual power that sets it aside from any other flawed human institution.

Part of the solution comes by understanding how God designed the church and the kingdom to relate. If we get this right, we will have powerful churches across the western world, churches which will provide an alternative and far preferable culture to that in which we presently live.

The kingdom of God is not like an earthly kingdom. It is not a piece of land with boundaries. It is completely outside of human grasp or control. The church is built through the exercise of God's kingdom power through us. Because the church is the only instrument God has chosen to advance his kingdom on earth, we have no choice but to access his kingdom power. The good news is that kingdom authority is given to the church. It was on the rock of the kingdom authority he had given to Peter that Jesus said he would build his church (Mt. 16:18).

The Jews were expecting a Messiah who would establish a literal kingdom on earth, a restored Davidic king who would rule the peoples of the world from a throne in Jerusalem. One of the most significant problems with dispensationalism (see the chapter on eschatology) is that it retains belief in this earthly kingdom, and then robs the kingdom from the church by locating its arrival in a future thousand-year rule of Christ on earth after the church has been removed.

This is not the kingdom that Jesus proclaimed. The kingdom he announced was both invisible and eternal: "The kingdom of God is not coming in ways that can be observed, nor will they say, 'Look, here it is!' or 'There!' for behold, the kingdom of God is in the midst of you" (Lk. 17:20-21). From the beginning of his ministry until after his resurrection, Jesus proclaimed the arrival of the kingdom of God: "The time is fulfilled, and the kingdom of God is at hand; repent and believe in the gospel" (Mk. 1:15). He sent out the twelve with the same mandate: "And proclaim as you go, saying, 'The kingdom of heaven is at hand'" (Mt. 10:8). He commanded the seventy-two: "Heal the sick in it and say to them, 'The kingdom of God has come near to you'" (Lk. 10:9). Wherever Jesus or the disciples preached the kingdom, signs and wonders of healing and deliverance followed. The power of the supernatural world was released as they stepped out in faith.

Jesus never equated the kingdom with his disciples. In Mt. 16:18-19, he said two things. First, the disciples were the church ("You are Peter, and on this rock I will build my church"). Second, the disciples would be given the keys of the kingdom ("I will give you the keys of the kingdom of heaven"). In other words, *the authority of the kingdom is given into the hands of the church.* In fact, *the kingdom creates the church.* At Pentecost, the presence of God's power released through the resurrection, expressed in the outpouring of the Holy Spirit, brought the church into being.

The kingdom of God, his eternal reign, existed before creation itself , let alone the church, and continues to exist once this world is ended. Yet the church retains a place of absolutely vital importance. *If the kingdom created the church, the church holds the keys of the kingdom.* The keys represent the power to lock or unlock the door. The locking or unlocking is done through our proclamation of the gospel. This does not mean that salvation comes about through our preaching. That is why Jesus said (literally): "I will give you the keys of the kingdom of heaven, and whatever you bind on earth shall have been bound in heaven, and whatever you loose on earth shall have been loosed in heaven" (Mt. 16:19). The preaching of the gospel unlocks what God has himself determined and enabled.

It is through the church that people enter the eternal kingdom. The church is indispensable as the only way into the kingdom, but the kingdom is indispensable as the only source of power for the church. So the two must work together. This has been a massive stumbling block for the church in our western rationalistic culture. We do not know how to to tap into the power of the kingdom, because we have great difficulty seeing into the world which exists beyond the confines of our five senses. Cessationism, the viewpoint that believes the age of miracles and gifts has passed (see chapter on prophecy), is little more than a justification of our unbelief. A church without access to supernatural power is at the mercy of an enemy who has no hesitation in exercising that kind of power against us.

Paul says this: "We look (*skopeo*) not to the things that are seen (*blepo*) but to the things that are unseen. For the things that are seen are transient, but the things that are unseen are eternal" (2 Cor. 4:18). He contrasts two Greek words for seeing. The first is *skopeo*, meaning to scrutinize or focus on, from which we get the word "scope," as in the scope of a rifle, telescope or microscope. The second word is *blepo*, the word for ordinary seeing. His point is that we can approach reality with ordinary natural vision, in which case we will be limited to what our five senses tell us. Or we can use our spiritual vision, our "scope," in which case we see that which cannot be seen by natural vision. Only this spiritual vision will enable us to gain access to the power of the kingdom.

Power is exercised in the natural world around us, by governments, police, judges, teachers, parents and all those in any place of authority. But power is also exercised in the unseen realm. The whole book of Revelation portrays the reality of divine and angelic help given to believers who are struggling and persecuted in this present world. Over and over again, the assurance is given them that they will be victorious. If all they see is what their five senses tell them, they will be tempted to give up, but as their eyes are opened, they see God is ruling over it all, and that his supernatural help is available to them. When we read to the end of the book, we find out that we win!

Paul prays that Christians may know "what is the immeasurable greatness of his power toward us who believe, according to the working of his great might that he worked in Christ when he raised him from the dead and seated him at his right hand in the heavenly places, far above all rule and authority and power and dominion"(Eph. 1:19-21). He prays "that I may know him and the power of his resurrection" (Phil. 3:10). To "know," according to the Bible, means to *know experientially*, not just to possess intellectual understanding. Paul wants us to experience and be convinced of the power of the resurrection. He wants us to know that the church operates by the power of the kingdom and that it must continually tap into that kingdom power.

Through the resurrection, God accomplished two things. He raised Christ from the dead and into a place of authority over all creation, and he made the power by which he did this available to every believer. This is the power of the kingdom. Look at what it did for the disciples. They went from fear to peace (Jn. 20:19-23). They went from unbelief to faith (Jn. 20:24-29). They went from nets that broke (Lk. 5:1-6) to nets that held the catch (Jn. 21:15-17). They went from failure to restoration (Jn. 21:15-17).

We understand the saving work of Christ on the cross and the need to receive forgiveness and be born again, but we do not adequately appreciate the power of the resurrection. We have Good Friday without Easter Sunday. We are placed into a battle in the seen world, but this battle will drag us down unless we tap into the power of the unseen world and claim it for ourselves. We are fighting an enemy with access to supernatural power, albeit a lesser power than God. There is a saving faith by which we confess Christ and are brought into the kingdom. But there is a persevering faith which we must exercise day by day. *Faith releases the power of the unseen into the seen.* Faith is neither an intellectual commodity nor an emotional feeling which we must possess in order to receive something from God. *Faith is simply the heart cry of the believer for the Father to equip him with the kingdom power we need to fight the battle we face.* We don't ask for possessions, material wealth or personal advancement, but we ask for what genuinely equips us to stand against the powers of darkness in boldness and courage, in order to persevere in the battle as long as it takes to win. We need the power of God.

This kingdom power is necessary if we are to see breakthroughs in the supernatural. But what we lose sight of is it is equally the power which enables us to persevere when things are tough, when finances are lousy, when relationships fall apart, when sickness strikes, when church splits occur, when people exhibit their fallen nature in church or out of it. At those times, we need the power of God to overcome. The overcomers in Revelation were those who persevered under persecution and refused to compromise their faith. Whether it is for miracles or for daily survival, we need the power of the kingdom.

And that is a power we can only access through personal relationship with the Father. Jesus found the power of the kingdom through his fellowship with the Father. He found the power to feed the five thousand, to give the blind their sight, to set the demonized free. But he also found it at Gethsemane, when the day was not for miracles but for carrying a Roman cross. He recognized that for the battle to be won, he needed the resources of the unseen world. He knew that the time he spent with the Father represented his access to that unseen world and to the heavenly power which places the enemy under our feet. However we choose to develop our personal fellowship with the Lord, we have to do it somehow if we expect to see battles fought and won in our own lives and in the world around us. If Jesus cried out for the resources only his heavenly Father could supply, how much more do we need to do so!

The charge brought against the first believers was that they were those who had caused trouble all over the world by proclaiming "another king" (Ac. 17:7). These believers not only spoke of salvation through the cross. They preached the kingdom of God. They insisted that God had come to rule among his people and over all the nations of the earth. They lived in the reality of this kingdom, working signs and wonders, enduring persecution and sharing Christ's love.

We need the power of this kingdom if the church in our culture is to fulfill the commission Jesus gave it to preach the gospel and disciple the nations. When the Holy Spirit came upon them at Pentecost, the disciples received power (Ac. 1:8). Paul said that the kingdom of God is not a matter of talk but of power (1 Cor. 4:20). The angelic voice declared to John: "Now the salvation and the power and the kingdom of our God and the authority of his Christ have come" (Rev. 12:10).

The kingdom of God comes in power, because it represents the supernatural authority of God himself. We have a battle to fight today, as the unseen power of evil draws people away after wealth, greed, immorality, false concepts of God and all the other deceptions the enemy can throw at us. Only the power of the kingdom will suffice for us to take our stand and see our neighbors, our work colleagues, our fellow students and our friends set free into the glorious liberty of the children of God.

This is why every believer is to pray as Jesus taught us: "Let your kingdom come, let your will be done." Let your kingdom, as it operates in the unseen world, become real here in the seen world. And as we pray, we must also be willing to become part of the answer to our prayers, as God empowers us as his representatives, ambassadors of his kingdom here on earth. There is no higher calling for the children of God. And no greater joy, as we see his resurrection power at work within us.

LAW AND GRACE

IS THE OLD TESTAMENT RELEVANT ANY MORE?

This seems to be a very strange question to ask Christians who believe in the Bible's authority. But think for a moment. Most of us have probably wondered about what importance the Old Testament has for us now that Christ has come and we are no longer under the authority of the law. Of course, we do not take scissors and cut the Old Testament out of our Bibles. But we might as well, for all the significance we often give to it. We tend to view the Old Testament as an outdated record of legalism, hypocrisy and failure, and then we wonder why we get so little out of our reading of it.

The problem arises out of a wrong understanding of the role of the law, and a failure to understand the deep interconnectedness of the Old and New Testaments. We believe that God gave the law with the goal that if people obeyed it perfectly by their own unaided efforts, they would earn eternal life. When this plan failed, owing to our sin, God offered the gospel instead. The problem with this understanding is that it portrays God as a deceiver. God knew that we could never obey the law perfectly. Why would he tantalize us with a promise he knew we could never reach?

THE TRAGEDY OF DISPENSATIONALISM

Part, though not all, of the reason we have fallen into such confusion about the Old Testament and the law is due to the influence of dispensationalism, particularly in North America (see chapter on eschalotogy). Dispensationalist teaching caused the church to move away from the understanding of the relationship of the two Testaments and of law and grace that had been accepted at least since the days of Augustine (354-430), if not before. Dispensationalists divided up the Bible into numerous "dispensations" or divisions of time. These dispensations were water-tight, and the way God related to humanity differed in each of them. Once the dispensation of the law was finished, the law had no further relevance. Not even the four Gospels apply to the Christian, because they are part of God's original plan to send Jesus to establish an earthly Jewish kingdom. That plan failed, and so the cross and the church constituted Plan B. The dispensation of grace in which we now live has nothing to do with the law, and is only an interlude until the millennium. Then, having removed the church, God will turn his attention back to his main goal, the establishment of an earthly Jewish kingdom, at which time the temple will be rebuilt and the law re-established. This mistaken view has affected people more than they probably realize.

As a result, we no longer understand the Bible as Jesus understood it. A gospel without the Old Testament is not the gospel Jesus preached. Does this re-introduce legalism? Not at all.

PROMISE AND FULFILMENT: THE UNITY OF THE OLD AND NEW TESTAMENTS

Contrary to the teaching of dispensationalism, a closer look at the Bible shows a remarkably close connection between the two Testaments. The Old Testament, just as much as the New Testament, teaches salvation by grace through faith in the promised Savior. The Bible contains only one promise of salvation and one means of salvation. God only ever had one plan.

A. ONE PROMISE OF SALVATION

The one promise of salvation runs throughout the entire Bible. This promise was given first to Adam and Eve immediately after the Fall. In Gen. 3:15, God warned the serpent that the seed of the woman would crush his head. In Genesis, unlike other Biblical genealogies, God specified the seed of the *woman*, not the *man*. This is because Jesus was born of a woman and without a human father. The seed passed down through the line of Seth through Noah and eventually to Abraham. The promise to Adam and Eve is reinforced in God's promise to Abraham that through his seed all the nations of the earth would be blessed (Gen. 22:18). At the time of the exodus, Moses prophesied concerning Christ (Deut. 18:15-19). The promise was passed down to King David, who prophetically spoke of Christ's body, as if it were his own, not being abandoned to the grave (Ps. 16:9-11). David also described the sufferings of Christ on the cross as if they were happening to him (Ps. 22:1-8).

The Old Testament promises, all fulfilled in the New Testament, go beyond the foretelling of Abraham's conquering descendant. Jeremiah promised a new covenant bringing forgiveness of sins and the renewing of the heart (Jer. 31:31-34). Isaiah promised that the servant of the Lord would bring an era of healing and forgiveness (Isa. 52:13-53:12). Ezekiel promised forgiveness, accompanied by the gift of the Spirit and of a new heart to enable God's people to fulfill his law (Ezek. 36:25-27). Joel promised the gift of the Spirit, accompanied by prophecy, visions and salvation (Joel 2:28-32). The New Testament doesn't bring a new promise. It brings the fulfilment of the promise already given.

B. ONE MEANS OF SALVATION

Why, if the law was meant to bring us justification through works, does the law itself teach that such a salvation is impossible? Paul points out that the law brings every person into accountability and judgment before a holy God, stating explicitly that none can be righteous before God by their own works (Rom. 3:19-20; Gal. 3:10). The law actually declares that justification by faith is the only way to life (Hab. 2:4, quoted in Gal. 3:11). The law was meant to be pursued not by works but by faith, and the Jews did not attain its goal because they tried to pursue it by works (Rom. 9:30-33). Paul urges the legalistic Galatians who want to pursue a righteousness from the law to listen to the testimony of the law itself concerning how the covenants relate to one another (Gal. 4:21-31). A large part of Hebrews (7:1-10:18) is designed to show that the sacrificial system of the Old Testament law is a foreshadowing of the sacrificial work of Christ. That is why Paul states in Rom. 3:21 that the law and the prophets *bear witness to* the righteousness of faith now revealed in Christ.

THE UNFOLDING PLAN OF GOD

We started this chapter by observing that we have often mistakenly viewed the Old Testament and the law as being outdated or irrelevant for Christians. But surely there are differences between the two Testaments? Surely there is a difference between the grace we have in Christ and the old way of serving God through the Mosaic law? Surely there is a sense in which the law is no longer applicable for Christians? The answer to all these questions is yes. But the way the purposes of God unfold can be described better as promise and fulfilment, rather than as something obsolete versus its replacement. The history of God's dealings with his people includes some things which were temporary, but at a deeper level he was drawing all things together as a foundation for the climax of his plan in Christ.

WHAT IS THE LAW?

When we think of the "law," the first thought that comes to mind is the series of sacrificial and ceremonial requirements given to Moses for the regulation of Israel's life as a nation. These do not seem to have any relevance to us as Christians today. The law did contain many such regulations, but it also included profound moral truths concerning love of God and neighbor. Indeed, in quoting Deut. 6:5 and Lev. 19:18, Jesus defined the heart of the law as the commandments to love God with all our heart and to love our neighbor as ourselves (Mt. 22:37-40). We also think of the law as referring only to the Pentateuch, the first five books of the Bible. Yet twice when Jesus quoted the law, he was actually quoting the Psalms (Jn. 10:34; 15:25). The same is true of Paul. In Rom. 3:10-20, he says that "the law" pronounces judgment upon the sins of all people, and illustrates this by eight quotations from Scripture, none of which come from the Pentateuch. By the time of Jesus, the full Hebrew title of what we call the Old Testament became "The law, the prophets and the writings," which was often shortened to "The law." It is only by context that we know when it uses the word "law" whether the New Testament is referring to the law of Moses or to some other portion of the Old Testament. Hebrews 7-10 seems to understand the law as both fulfilled and replaced by the sacrifice of Christ on the cross. But Hebrews refers particularly to that aspect of the law of Moses dealing with the sacrificial system, rather than those parts dealing with timeless moral truths. So it seems that there are two senses of the word, a narrower sense referring only to the sacrificial and ceremonial aspect of the law of Moses, and a wider sense referring to the whole of the Old Testament revelation, of which love of God and neighbor is at the heart.

THE PURPOSE OF THE LAW

According to the New Testament, the law has a number of purposes. We can divide these into two groups. The first group describes the functions of the law in relation to the exposing and judging of human sin. The second group describes the functions of the law in relation to its preparing us for and leading us to the Savior.

The first category could be described as a "negative" in nature and deals with sin:

- The law defines sin as disobedience to God.

- It then sharpens that definition by transforming sin into transgression, illuminating the whole range of human conduct as wilful violation of God's commands.

- It exposes the heart of legalism, in which sin masquerades as self-exalting religious ritualism.

- It pronounces the entirely righteous and just judgment of God upon all human sin, leaving no person exempt or excused.

The second category could be described as "positive" in nature and deals with preparation:

- The law prepares us for Christ by promising and prophesying his coming.

- The law prepares us for Christ by showing his perfect obedience to its commands.

- The law prepares us for Christ by showing how his obedience contrasts with our own disobedience, showing us that our only hope of fulfilling the law is to be found in him.

- The law prepares us for Christ through its sacrificial system which provides a measure of forgiveness while pointing to full forgiveness in Christ.

THE FULFILMENT OF THE LAW

The law thus leads us to Christ, sin's solution. But now that Christ has come, does the law have any continuing role? The answer is to be found in the declaration of Jesus: "Do not think that I have come to abolish the Law or the Prophets; I have not come to abolish them but to fulfill them. For truly, I say to you, until heaven and earth pass away, not an iota, not a dot, will pass from the Law until all is accomplished. Therefore whoever relaxes one of the least of these commandments and teaches others to do the same will be called least in the kingdom of heaven, but whoever does

them and teaches them will be called great in the kingdom
of heaven. For I tell you, unless your righteousness exceeds
that of the scribes and Pharisees, you will never enter the
kingdom of heaven" (Mt. 5:17-20).

Jesus teaches here that the law comes to its fulfillment in
himself. Only in him is any true fulfillment of the law
possible. Up till now, humanity has stood under the curse
of sin and legalism, but now the way is opened for a true
obedience to the law to take place. In the kingdom of heaven,
which broke into this world when Jesus began his ministry
and comes to its fulfillment in the new Jerusalem, there
will be a true obedience to God's law. The nature of this
obedience will correspond to our own condition. On earth
it will be limited, though genuine, while in heaven it will
be perfect, as we will be transformed fully into the likeness
of Christ. We cannot enter into this kingdom without the
gift of God's righteousness in Christ. Through Christ our
righteousness – or more accurately, Christ's righteousness
in us – will far surpass the self-made righteousness of the
Pharisees and teachers of the law.

But how is the law fulfilled in Christ? We find it fulfilled
in two ways:

**1. Christ's sacrifice on the cross fulfils the law by bringing
the sacrificial system to its climax and conclusion, so that
we now relate to God through Christ's sacrifice rather**

than the sacrifice of animals. We all know that, thankfully, we do not have to bring an animal for sacrifice every time the church gathers together! The reason for this is explained in Hebrews 7-10. The sacrificial system had no power to bring people to righteousness. In that connection it is described as weak and useless (Heb. 7:18). Now Christ has come, a perfect High Priest offering a perfect sacrifice (Heb. 7:26-28). Christ's sacrifice has obtained an eternal redemption (9:12) and the forgiveness of sins (9:28). Now that Christ has come, God has set aside the first system of sacrifice by the once-for-all perfect sacrifice of his Son (10:9). The practical consequence of this is that all those aspects of the law which deal with the attaining of external purification, including the dietary laws, are ended in Christ, through whom we have now received true purification of the heart. Jesus himself confirmed this when he told the Pharisees that what comes out of a man's heart is what makes him unclean, not what enters into his mouth (Mk. 7:17-23). Mark saw in this comment that Jesus was declaring the imminent end of the ceremonial aspect of the law: "Thus he declared all foods clean" (Mk. 7:19). The apostles realized this at the Jerusalem Council (Ac. 15:5-21) when they saw that it was not right to require Gentile believers to be circumcised, as circumcision represented the ceremonial aspect of the law. Jewish believers (including Paul, see Ac. 16:3; 22:26) carried on observing aspects of the ceremonial law in order not to give offence to the Jewish community and undermine their witness, but even this ceased with the destruction of the temple. Paul told the Galatians that if they believe we must be circumcised in order to be saved, we are re-instituting justification by works rather than by the grace of God (Gal. 5:2-6).

2. Christ's sacrifice on the cross fulfils the law by making possible for the first time a measure of genuine obedience to its commands. Jesus saw that the heart of the law did not lie in the sacrificial or ritual purity system, which he knew would come to an end by his sacrificial death. When asked what the greatest commandment in the law was, he replied by quoting Deut. 6:5 and Lev. 19:18: "You shall love the Lord your God with all your heart and with all your soul and with all your mind. This is the great and first commandment. And the second is like it: You shall love your neighbor as yourself. On these two commandments depend all the Law and the Prophets" (Mt. 22:37-39). Jesus did not come to bring a new law. He came to show the meaning of the law in its truest sense by living out a life of perfect obedience to its commands. Only in the life of Christ do we see these great commandments of the law walked out in a way that displays their deepest significance. There is therefore no conflict between obedience to the law and the command we are given as Christians to "walk as Jesus did" (1 Jn. 2:6). They are in fact one and the same thing. The teaching of the New Testament is thus an exposition of the law in the light of the coming of Christ and of his sinless life.

Jesus did not come to bring us a new ethic. His teaching on love was drawn from the way love is carefully defined in the

Old Testament. His goal was to show us how to obey the law. He did this in two ways: first, by teaching us the true meaning of the law in light of its greatest commandments; and second, by showing us practically in his life what perfect obedience to the law looks like. How could we understand the depth of the command to love our neighbor unless we heard it explained from Jesus' lips and saw it in his life? In the Sermon on the Mount, Jesus interpreted the law and drew out its true intent in a way that had been obscured and twisted by the Pharisees. He told the people repeatedly: "You have heard *that*... but I tell you *this*" (Mt. 5:21, 27, 31,33, 38, 43). What the people "have heard" is not the true intent of the law, but its legalistic perversion in the hands of the Pharisees. They had reduced the radical demands of the law to external obligations they could fulfil and thus advertise their own righteousness. Jesus returned the law to its original meaning (5:32), a meaning so all-encompassing in its implications we could never claim to be able to fulfil it by our own efforts. For instance, while commending the Pharisees for their meticulous tithing, he rebuked them for failing to practice the deeper matters of the law — the justice, mercy and faithfulness which form the basis for why we tithe (Mt. 23:23-24).

Paul has exactly the same view. He never says that the law is abolished. The righteousness of God revealed in Christ is testified to by the law (Rom. 3:21), and in return God's righteousness in Christ upholds or establishes the law (Rom.

3:31). Because of what Christ did on the cross, the believer has died with him and is no longer subject to the law's just condemnation of his sin. This does not mean that the law is abolished, or that the believer has no further relationship with it. What it does mean is that now the believer *relates to the law in a different way.* Jesus has come and has fulfilled those requirements for us while at the same time giving us his Spirit. This means that, for the first time, we can begin to fight back successfully against the power of sin and produce a genuine, though imperfect, measure of obedience to the law. Paul's longing to obey God's law (Rom. 7:22) is enabled by the empowering of the Holy Spirit, who through Christ has set him free from the law's just condemnation of his sin (Rom. 8:1-2). The goal of God's work in Christ is that now, for the first time, the righteous requirement of his law might be met in those who walk by the power of the Spirit (Rom. 8:4). Previously, the law stood against us as a just but condemning judge. Now, it comes as an inspiring encouragement to be like Christ. Instead of encountering the commandment as a "Thou shalt *not*," where we never reached the standard, we now encounter it as "Thou *shalt* not," where God gives us the ability to obey.

Some try to say the Old Testament law and the Christian ethic of love are two different things. They say we are no longer called to obey the law, but simply to act in love. But how is this "love" to be defined? Love without definition quickly becomes a licence to tolerate anything. A commitment to uphold Biblical standards rapidly becomes judged as "unloving" or "intolerant." Along with the Bible, we must insist that *love has defined content*. Paul understood it exactly this way, as these words show: "Owe no one anything, except to love each other, for the one who loves another has fulfilled the law. For the commandments, 'You shall not commit adultery, You shall not murder, You shall not steal, You shall not covet,' and any other commandment, are summed up in this word: 'You shall love your neighbor as yourself.' Love does no wrong to a neighbor; therefore love is the fulfilling of the law" (Rom. 13:8-10). Why is it he says we are to owe no one anything, *except* the ongoing debt of love? The reason is given in the next statement: anyone who completely fulfils the requirement to love has completely obeyed the law (verse 8). Such a thing is not possible in this life, which is *why the debt will always remain outstanding*. Paul goes through a sampling of the commandments, saying they are representative of all the law's commands (verse 9). All these commands are "summed up" in the one command to love our neighbor. *That the law is summed up in love means that each individual command of the moral law is motivated by love.* Love (of God and neighbor) is the golden thread which runs through all the commands of the Old Testament – whether they deal with honoring God's name or not removing a neighbor's boundary stone. Love is not a new revelation Jesus brought. Love is the heart of the law, now fully understood in Christ by revelation of the Spirit (2 Cor. 3:15-16), which God enables us to walk out by the Spirit's power. Love, as Paul concludes here (Rom. 13:10), is the fulfilling of the law. When we truly love God and neighbor, we are fulfilling the righteous requirement of God's law, whether that be not to commit adultery, murder, steal, covet or to obey any other command.

The height of Paul's argument concerning the law is reached in Rom. 10:4, where he declares that Christ is the goal (*telos*) of the law. The Jews' mistake was to pursue the law as if it were meant to be obeyed by works they themselves performed in order to establish their own righteousness (Rom. 9:31-33). But God designed the law precisely to show the impossibility of any such attempt. The law showed men and women their sinfulness (Rom. 3:9-20) and their inadequacy in comparison to the holiness of God (Rom. 7:7-13). The Greek word *telos* in Rom. 10:4 has a wide range of meaning — everything from "goal" or "purpose," to "fulfilment" or "maturity," to "end" or "cessation." The context, however, shows that "goal" is the meaning Paul intends here. How could he speak of Christ as the cessation of the law when he has repeatedly spoken of him as bringing about the law's establishment (Rom. 3:31) and the performing of its requirements by the Spirit (Rom. 8:4), the standard the Gentiles reached when they approached the law by faith, not by works (Rom. 9:30)?

But what about the other places where Paul seems to reject the law as no longer relevant to us? Let's look at each of those briefly.

Galatians. In Galatia, Paul was fighting a group of legalists who appear to have exalted the law above Christ. Even though the law comes to its fulfillment in Christ, the law is only Christ's servant. These legalists suggested that people could be justified by their own works or by religious rituals, rather than by faith in Christ. Paul must safeguard the truth of the Gospel. He does so by emphasizing the negative aspect of the law's role (in exposing sin) rather than the positive aspect (the law fulfilled in Christ). This is a much narrower focus than in Romans, yet there is no conflict between the two. That no one can be justified by the works of the law (Gal. 2:16) underlines humanity's sinfulness, not something wrong in the law. In fact, the law is not at all opposed to the promises of God (Gal. 3:21). The law cannot give life by itself, as the legalists suppose, but rather it declares all people are sinners and therefore leads them to Christ (3:21-22). There is no conflict here with Paul's teaching in Romans. Those who wish to be "under the law" (that is, to be justified by their own works) are in conflict with the teaching of the law itself (4:21), which shows prophetically that the present-day Jewish legalists are descendants of Hagar, whereas those Jews and Gentiles who have found in Christ the fulfilment of the law are descendants of Sarah and of the promise to Abraham (4:21-31). Again, no conflict with Romans. In 3:19, Paul says regarding the law's purpose that it was "added because of transgressions" until the promised Seed had come. Paul points out simply that the law came after Abraham and that one of its purposes was to define transgression by shining a light on the holiness of God and on our failure to obey him. Paul chooses not to elaborate on the positive aspects of the law's purpose for fear that the Galatian legalists might seize on and distort his words. The Galatians need to stop seeing the law as independent of or exalted over Christ and come back into Biblical balance.

2 Corinthians 3. Here Paul presents a contrast not between law and gospel, but between two *ministries* – that of Moses and that of the ministers of the new covenant. The Corinthians themselves are letters written by the Spirit on tablets of human hearts, not tablets of stone (verses 1-3). In the new covenant, the law is written on the hearts of people, *not just* on tablets of stone. Paul is thinking of Jer. 31:31-34: under the new covenant the law, far from being abolished, will be written on our hearts. Under the old covenant, the letter killed, but under the new covenant, the Spirit gives life (verse 6). This must be understood properly. Paul's contrasting of "letter" and Spirit" does not contrast law and gospel. It contrasts *two understandings of the law,* just as in Rom. 9:30-33. The "letter" is not the law as God gave it, but the law misunderstood as an instrument to achieve our own righteousness. But by the Spirit we come to a proper understanding of the law, the true fulfilling of the law as in Rom. 8:4. The ministry of Moses holds a limited glory (verse 9). *This tell us that we no longer relate to the law through Moses, but through Christ.* When we turn to the Spirit (verses 16-

17), we come to a true understanding of the old covenant, an understanding our human sinfulness had blinded us to. The veil (not the law) is now removed, and we can see the true meaning of the old covenant clearly (verse 14) as leading to Christ. Paul's argument here is completely in line with what his says in Romans.

Eph. 2:14-18. In verse 15, Paul says Christ made peace between Jew and Gentile "by abolishing the law of commandments expressed in ordinances." Yet in Eph. 6:2, Paul quotes Deut. 5:16 as being valid today for Christians. If he is teaching in chapter 2 that the law is abolished, he is in conflict not only with what he is saying in Romans, but with what he is saying later in the same letter! The context in Eph. 2:11-22 deals with how the Old Testament law separated the Gentiles from the Jews. He divides the law into two aspects. First, he speaks negatively of circumcision (verse 11), which stands for the whole sacrificial and ceremonial aspect of the law now fulfilled by Christ. But next he refers to the "covenants of the promise" (verse 12), speaking of the law in its positive sense. The Gentiles were previously excluded from these covenants and thus without hope and without God (verse 12). The Gentiles have now come into possession of the promise contained in the law and are included in that covenant grace of God which has made them citizens and no longer foreigners (verse 19). Christ has destroyed the "dividing wall of partition, that is, the enmity," between Jew and Gentile, and he has done this by destroying "the law of commandments expressed in ordinances." This is an unusual phrase. The law is qualified twice: it is the "law of commandments," and "the law expressed in ordinances." Paul is making clear that he is not referring to the law in its entirety. He is referring to a specific aspect of the law, the sacrificial and ceremonial system. In particular, he is referring to circumcision, which he has referred to in verse 11 as typifying the division between Jew and Gentile. This aspect of the law was what ruled the national life of Israel when that nation alone held possession of the covenant promises of God. *This aspect* of the law, *not* the law as an expression of the promise of God (verse 12), *nor* the law as an expression of the moral character of God still authoritative for Christians (6:2), is what constitutes the dividing wall between Jew and Gentile, which is now brought down in Christ.

Col. 2:14. Paul says here that Christ forgave our sins "by canceling the record of debt that stood against us with its legal demands. This he set aside nailing it to the cross." Paul is not referring to the law. The "record of debt" is a *cheirographon*. This is the Greek word for an "IOU," something written by one's own hand, often in wax, in the form of an oath or bond. This debt, with its "legal demands" (the particulars of what was owed), is now cancelled (literally "smeared away," as one would smear away something written in wax). A real *cheirographon*, interestingly, appears in the New Testament in the form of Paul's letter to Philemon. The IOU Paul refers to in Col. 2:14 is the statement of debt each of us, Jew or Gentile, owes to God and cannot repay. That is why it "stands against us," and requires the cross of Christ to cancel it. God forgives us this debt because Christ has paid its price in full. This verse is a beautiful word picture of what Christ has done for us, but it has nothing in fact to do with the law.

1 Tim. 1:8-11. In this passage, Paul states that the law is made not for good people but for lawbreakers, rebels, murderers and so on. This might suggest that the law has no relevance for Christians. But note the context. Paul is criticizing those who are *misusing* the law to turn believers away from true doctrine and into myths and genealogies. No wonder he describes them as "desiring to be teachers of the law, without understanding either what they are saying or the things about which they make confident assertions" (verse 7). These false teachers are turning people away from Christ and, under the pretense of teaching the law, are introducing myths and others teachings that have nothing to do with the law at all. Paul points out in verses 8-11 that the law has a proper role in exposing human sin and bringing them under the just judgment of God. As in Galatians, he restricts himself to noting this negative aspect of the law's role because of the nature of the heresy he is fighting, not wanting to give ammunition to his opponents by enlarging on the positive role of the law in the believer's life.

THE UNBREAKABLE VALIDITY OF GOD'S COVENANT

Archaeological records show us that in the middle-eastern world of the second millennium BC (the time of Moses), conquering kings used a clearly-defined treaty format to impose their will on defeated peoples. This would have been the way the people of Israel understood for a people to come into submission to a king. The covenant (or treaty) God made with Moses and the children of Israel more or less exactly follows this format. God takes the place of the conquering king and Israel are the people he conquers or asserts his rulership over. God used a vehicle for his revelation which would have been easily and clearly understood by all the people. The heart of this covenant (and of our Old Testament) is the Mosaic law, but it is not hard to see how the other parts of the Old Testament are related to it. Pre-mosaic history (Genesis) sets the stage for the delivery of the covenant by defining who God is and who his people are, as well as illuminating God's character and faithfulness. Post-mosaic history (historical books) is a record of obedience or disobedience to the Mosaic covenant. The Psalms are largely the worship accompaniment to the covenant celebrations (whether daily or weekly rituals or the great festivals). The prophetic books contain God's warnings regarding disobedience to the covenant in subsequent times. The wisdom books (Proverbs, Ecclesiastes) bring practical application of the covenant to various areas of life. The various parts of the Old Testament operate in unity to form God's ongoing conduct of his covenantal relationship with his people.

The ancient treaty was a binding agreement between two parties (with copies to both). It came in written form, could not be abrogated or altered, and had promises and curses attached. This is the form the Mosaic covenant and Old Testament take, and this is the foundation of their authority. Such a treaty, once given, constituted a permanent, unchangeable legal document governing the relationship of the conquering king with the conquered people. Likewise, the Mosaic covenant (and, by extension, the entire Old Testament) was a permanent legal document detailing the requirements God placed upon his people. As with the ancient treaties, curses were attached to those who would alter the covenant document in any way (Deut. 4:2).

Thus God himself fashioned the Old Testament as a permanently-binding and authoritative expression of his will, down to the last detail, even though he utilized humanly-understandable forms to express it. The ancient treaties show us exactly how the people of Israel would have easily comprehended the meaning of God's covenant as they received it, and why they held the Scriptures in such high reverence. This also explains why, even as other ancient treaties had to be preserved and guarded in a secure and often sacred location, the Mosaic covenant had to be preserved in the ark of the covenant. It explains why Moses wrote two copies of the covenant (Deut. 4:13, which has sometimes been misunderstood as one copy written on two stones), one for God and the other for Israel. Finally, it explains why the whole Old Testament was so meticulously passed down for well over a millennium in a society without printing presses! Covenant requires Scripture —

where there is covenant, there will without doubt be a binding written record of its terms and conditions, and that is what the Bible is. You cannot have faith in the God of the Bible without possessing and obeying his written record of covenant. This is the foundation for our understanding of the authority of Scripture. The Bible is authoritative, therefore, not because the church says it is but because God has inspired and created it himself, and it holds validity independent of any human agency or power.

THIS CONCEPT ALSO EXPLAINS THE AUTHORITY OF THE NEW COVENANT IN CHRIST

What about the New Testament? The New Testament is fundamentally a renewal of the Old Testament covenant. It is given by the same God, and its conditions are prophesied in the original covenant from Genesis to Malachi. Moses, as well as Abraham and David, not to mention the prophets, spoke of the coming of the Messiah. The Old Testament, indeed, is in its entirety a prophetic foreshadowing of the

New. The New Testament renews the Mosaic covenant, but alters its conditions, so that forgiveness comes by the blood of Christ rather than temple sacrifices. It also alters the nature of the covenant community, widening it from Jews to people of all nations. The structure of the New Testament is amazingly similar to that of the Old. At its heart is the giving of the covenant in Christ. Like the Old Testament, it has its history which sets the stage (Gospels), as well as a historical record of the subsequent obedience and disobedience of the covenant community (Acts and Letters), contains prophetic insight and teaching (Letters, including Revelation), wisdom (Letters) and worship (Letters and Revelation). This new covenant, being a renewal of the old, has the same characteristics of the latter, in that it comes from God, is inviolable and cannot be altered, and (just as in Deut. 4:2) even has curses attached to that end (Rev. 22:18-19). Jesus summed it up: "Scripture cannot be broken" (Jn. 10:35).

COVENANT AND CULTURE: THE WAR WE FACE

Wherever the values of the pagan culture around us conflict with those of the Bible, we come under pressure and are tempted to compromise. But how can we persuade God's people to compromise when the Bible is so clear? If we appear openly to be undermining the Bible's authority, we know that warning signals will come on. So instead the concept of cultural relativity is introduced. That is, certain parts of the Bible were relevant to the culture in which they were written, but not to our own. This enables us to say the Bible is authoritative, while at the same time denying its authority for us. It also ignores the fact that Biblical values were just as radically counter-cultural in the pagan environment of the first century as they are to in the pagan environment of today. It is heresy to say that parts of Scripture are only "culturally relevant" and not authoritative for us today. The Bible is either authoritative or it is not. The only parts of Scripture which are no longer to be observed are those parts *which Scripture itself teaches* are not to be observed – such as the daily offering of bulls and presentation of other sacrifices. Just because a teaching of Scripture is offensive to modern culture does not give that culture the right to declare those teachings out of date. The entire doctrine of the Atonement – the sacrificial death of Christ on the cross – is based on what are (humanly speaking) completely outdated Jewish cultural concepts of animal sacrifice. As Christians, we understand that such sacrifices are no longer to be offered, not because they are outdated or culturally unacceptable, but because God himself has substituted another sacrifice for these, the sacrifice of his own Son. But the sacrifice of Christ on the cross makes no sense outside of the Old Testament understanding of the power of sacrifice to satisfy the anger of a holy God – a concept completely foreign to our modern culture. Once we discard this "outdated" concept of sacrifice, we have discarded the cross itself. When we begin to pick and choose which parts of Scripture are acceptable to us, it will not be long before we have thrown out Scripture – and our faith – completely. Such is proved by the history of modern theology, which began with the rejecting of "minor" points, and ended, several generations later, with the rejection of everything else. If you don't believe me, look at the history of mainline Protestant denominations, almost every one of which is projected to become extinct within the very near future. Why newer Christian movements want to go down that road is a mystery to me. It is theological and spiritual suicide.

Our job is not to make peace with the pagan culture and the demonic forces behind it. Our job is to stand fast on the truth of the unbreakable covenant God has made with his people. He will honor our obedience. Like the persecuted believers of the seven churches of Revelation, we may suffer politically, economically and socially. But God will keep us spiritually safe. Any gains we make in this world by compromise are transient and worthless by comparison with the eternal losses we will suffer. It is always worth it to persevere. God is faithful to his covenant, and he will not abandon those who hold fast to it.

The words of the psalmist still ring true: "Great peace have those who love your law; nothing can make them stumble" (Ps. 119:165).

THE CHURCH

The local church is the visible face of Christianity everywhere in the world except where Christians are persecuted and have to go underground.

The church, according to our chapter on the kingdom, is God's indispensable instrument through which Jesus meets an unsaved world. Christ gave the church the keys to the kingdom, and it is only through the church that people enter it.

On the surface, the church seems to be in a state of upheaval throughout the western world. People float from one place of fellowship to another, or leave the church entirely, often thinking they can maintain a Christian commitment without it. There are many ideas about what church should be, yet often these ideas seem anything but rooted in Biblical truth. Churches are closing, churches are opening, and churches are treading water.

In one sense, it has never been much different. Christians who point back to the first century church as a model have forgotten all the difficulties it had. John wrote to seven churches in Asia. The number, as all others in Revelation, is symbolic. Seven is the number of completion and of God. The seven churches represent God's church in every age. Of the seven, three were treading water, two were in serious trouble and two were commended as faithful. That's probably a fair ratio of where local churches in any given locality or season are at.

But that's no reason to give up on the great purposes God has for the church. Christians live in a tension between the *real* (where we are at) and the *ideal* (where God is calling us to). We will never reach the ideal in this life, but the existence of the ideal pulls us out of the real, the place where we're presently at but shouldn't remain in.

If the church is the only instrument God chose for the extension of his kingdom, the stakes in getting things right about it could not be higher.

Setting aside for a moment our personal preconceptions, can we drill down and find some Biblical bedrock to build our spiritual house upon?

THE BODY OF CHRIST

It may seem an obvious point to make, but we still need to make it: the church is people, not buildings. The old covenant was build around a holy place, the temple. The new covenant is built around a holy people, the church. Never refer to a church building as the church! Our terminology can reveal our theology. Is our thinking old covenant or new covenant? It does make a difference, because there are lots of people who feel that we don't have a real church until we have a building. Sometimes we need buildings, but sometimes we don't. Buildings are accessories, not necessities. They are our servants, not our masters. We should acquire one if we have a real need for it, if we can't function properly without it, and if it does not consume resources that should be going into people. Buildings, even ones God has provided, carry a tendency to warp our theology by making us think of the church more as an institution and less as a family. It's easy to appreciate the church is people when you don't have a building, but when you do have one, you have to keep this truth in front of you and never lose sight of it.

The church is not a building, but it does have a structure. It is not just a crowd gathered together for no purpose. The New Testament gives a very specific form to the structure of the church: it is the *body of Christ*. The church is never called simply "a body," but always a "body in Christ" (Rom. 12:5) or "the body of Christ" (1 Cor. 12:27; Eph. 4:12). In other words, the church receives its significance as a body or corporate reality *only in its relationship to Jesus Christ.* Every other human family, organization, society or nation is related on a purely human or natural basis. Only the church is constituted on the basis of its relationship to Christ: "For just as the body is one and has many members, and all the members of the body, though many, are one body, so it is with Christ" (1 Cor. 12:12). We would have expected Paul to end this statement on the body with "so it is with the church," which would nicely make his point comparing the church to the human body. But, even though his topic is unity in the church, he ends the statement instead with "so it is with Christ." What he means is that the body which is the church is not just the church as a group of people, but is really part of Christ himself. This statement, though familiar to our ears, must have been stunning to those who first read it.

The significance and value of each person is determined only in relation to Christ. Christ has placed each member in the body, and this is why the body cannot function properly without each member being healthy and valued.

That is why the church, as an organization, is completely unlike any other human entity. In fact, it is not so much an *organization* as it is an *organism* – a network of relationships rooted in the relationship of each member with Christ. It is not built with a view to making the leaders look good or even make the organization appear outwardly successful. It is built instead on the foundation of the infinite worth and value of each of its members – and this in turn affects how it views and treats those yet outside its boundaries for whom Christ has also died.

The idea of the church as the body of Christ speaks to the issue of unity. Our unity is determined not by our relationship with one another, but by our common relationship with Christ. As the piano is tuned not on the basis of the relationship of each note to the next, but on the common relationship of all notes to the tuning fork, so it is with the church. Our unity is not even based on allegiance to a statement of faith or common set of doctrines, although part of obedience to Christ is obedience to his Word and to its unquestionable and final authority in our lives. Our unity is based on our common relationship to Christ and the fact he has made all of us members of his body, and therefore members of one another. That is why the church can bring together people who would never ordinarily relate to one another – people of every race, class, educational level and personality type.

The first picture we get of the church is in Ac. 2:43-47: "And they devoted themselves to the apostles' teaching and the fellowship, to the breaking of bread and the prayers. And awe came upon every soul, and many wonders and signs were being done through the apostles. And all who believed were together and had all things in common. And they were selling their possessions and belongings and distributing the proceeds to all, as any had need. And day by day, attending the temple together and breaking bread in their homes, they received their food with glad and generous hearts, praising God and having favor with all the people. And the Lord added to their number day by day those who were being saved."

It isn't that God wants us to try to replicate the experience of first-century churches, for their experience, like ours, was mixed. But this first Christian fellowship, flowing out of a shared life in the Spirit, birthed in the history-making moments of Pentecost, has several lessons to teach us.

The church is a place of community. The basis of their community was their faith in Christ: they are described simply as those who believed. Believers are those who have believed in or trusted Christ. The Greek verb *pisteuo* refers not to an intellectual belief but to the trusting of a person. When we believe, we entrust our lives and our destiny, now and forever, to Jesus Christ, and we enter into personal relationship with him. All other religions are based on *beliefs about God*, but only Christianity is based on a *relationship with God*.

As we read this passage, we could easily pass over the comment that believers were "together." Yet it is significant. Believers should want to be together.   Fellowship is something we should long for. The church is meant to be the place where people find community. They even had "all things in common." This doesn't mean they lived communally, but that they were ready to sell their possessions to give to others as the need arose. Roman writers were amazed by the fact that the Christians were the only people who had no poor among them. True community places God and others first, living out the two most important commandments of the law. They met together daily for worship and even to eat together. Later on, the New Testament tells us that the whole church gathered regularly on the first day of the week (Ac. 20:7; 1 Cor. 16:1-4), but there is no reason to believe they did not also continue to fellowship together through the week. We complain about having to gather once a week to worship, fellowship and be taught, but believers in the first church wanted to be together as much as possible. Our corporate gatherings are mandated by Scripture. If we don't feel like going, we need to look at what's wrong with our hearts which causes us to turn away from fellowship, or we need to look at what's wrong with our gatherings, and then take steps to restore both our hearts and gatherings to what God intends them to be. Believers should enjoy each other's company and want to be together.

The church should be the best place in the world to find community. But community requires that we share our lives with others. This is not a matter of personality types. It is far deeper than that. Where the love of Christ is truly present amongst his people, everyone will want to be there.

The church is a place of commitment. These believers are described as "devoted." The Greek verb *proskartereo* means in a literal sense to be glued or stuck together. In a word, they were committed. And their commitment extended in four directions.

They were committed to the apostles' teaching. We are a people of the Word. People only get tired of teaching when the teaching strays from its source of life in Scripture. We should be less seeker-sensitive and more Word-sensitive. Believers committed to Biblical teaching allow the Word of God to judge the culture, never vice-versa. We do not cut parts out of the Bible because they offend the culture we live in. We cut parts out of the culture because they offend the Bible. If believers were devoted to the apostles' teaching, they were also then devoted to the apostles themselves. They expressed their loyalty to God in a strong willingness to follow the leaders he had appointed over them. Without this kind of commitment to leadership, no church can move ahead. God created the world with a definite order, and part of this order is submission to those in authority – whether children to parents, wives to husbands, employees to employers or citizens to government. Why should we think that respect for church leaders is an exception? Leaders must act as servants, even as Christ did, but they must be free to lead.

They were committed to the fellowship. They possessed a bond of commitment, loyalty and faithfulness without which a New Testament church is impossible to build. This commitment is described here in a literal sense as the glue which holds the church together. Being in the church is a little like being married. We walk together in a covenant bond which expresses our commitment to stick with and to each other no matter what. An interesting thing happens when people express this kind of covenant commitment. They receive a sense of significance and value. When the church is operating properly, everyone in it finds worth and value. Just as Paul says, the parts of the body we think are less honorable we treat with special honor, that every part should have equal concern for each other (1 Cor. 12:23-25).

They were committed to the breaking of bread. This word is used both for common meals and the fellowship involved in them, and also for the Lord's Supper. There is no contradiction in this, for in the New Testament the Lord's Supper was always observed within the context of a common meal. They enjoyed being together and sharing fellowship, and they enjoyed celebrating what Christ had done for them. Communion is not meant to be a religious ritual, but a celebration of the sacrifice which made community possible.

And finally, they were committed to prayer. No church can grow strong and deep unless believers develop and maintain a heart for prayer. Prayer is the lifeblood of our relationship with the Lord. The quality of its members' relationship with the Lord will ultimately determine the success and health of any local church.

The church is a place of power. "Awe" or fear (the Greek word is *phobos*) came on all those who witnessed the signs and wonders characteristic of the first church. When we see a mighty phenomenon in nature, we draw back in a measure of fear – which is why few people attempt to go over Niagara Falls in a barrel! How much more should we rightly fear when we witness the awesome power of God? Later in Acts we read the same phenomenon was continuing: "Now many signs and wonders were regularly done among the people by the hands of the apostles... And more than ever believers were added to the Lord, multitudes of both men and women, so that they even carried the sick into the streets and laid them on cots and mats, that as Peter came by at least his shadow might fall on some of them" (Ac. 5:12-15). Godly fear motivates us to express our love through obedience and true worship. A church moving in the power of the Spirit and receiving the outpouring of his amazing love should never fail also to live in a true and righteous fear of God. And when the fear of God falls on those who do not know the Lord, it becomes a doorway to revival. The church in our western culture has far too long drunk from the well of rationalism without even knowing it. We have lived in practice on the basis that miracles are next to impossible rather than normal. We believe in a supernatural God and a supernatural presence of his Spirit, but that belief has not invaded the day to day outworking of our faith. We need to repent for accepting the idea that modern western science and rationalism is the highest form of wisdom. We need to return to a Biblical worldview. When Paul said the gospel is the power of God for salvation, he did not mean to restrict that power to God's ability to draw us to Christ. The gospel is advanced by the exercise of the power of God, whether that be in preaching or in signs and wonders. Until those signs and wonders are seen again, our churches will not experience the breakthroughs that through Paul and others brought the gospel to the far reaches of the Roman Empire within a few short years.

DISCIPLESHIP: THE BIBLICAL PRESCRIPTION FOR A HEALTHY CHURCH

In the opening chapters of his gospel, Matthew lays out a clear distinction between two groups. There were the large crowds of people who appeared wherever Jesus was. But there was also the much smaller band of disciples who traveled with him. He called Peter, Andrew, James and John to leave everything behind and follow him (4:18-22).

But the next verses (23-25) tell of the "great crowds" that mobbed him wherever he went. Nowhere is it suggested that Jesus made the same demands of the crowds that he made of the disciples. Nowhere is it suggested that the crowds left everything behind and followed Jesus all over Galilee. They were local people who just appeared wherever he was, and then went back to their daily lives. Jesus' strategy was not to focus on large numbers, but to work with a small group whom he discipled to reach the large numbers.

Why is it that in church today we so often seek the opposite? We love to create big churches where many are entertained, but few are equipped. People come and go, untrained, untaught and undiscipled. Instead, we should be working with small groups of disciples, teaching and training them to create a spiritual families who will go out, plant churches and create more disciples. Crowds will disperse in a minute. Families last for a lifetime.

Jesus never built his church on the crowds. He built it on the small group of disciples. He didn't study the demographics, create a trendy brand and open a coffee shop in the foyer. He said this: "You are Peter, and on this rock I will build my church" (Mt. 16:18). We can reach out to the crowds if we move in miracles and gifts of healing as Jesus did, but the crowds should never form the foundation of our church, any more than they formed the foundation of his. They are, at best, a fishing pond from which we can draw disciples.

Jesus reached out to the crowds in compassion, but always chose to build his church on the much smaller foundation of those willing to give up everything to follow him. We should do the same today if we want to be successful in building the church Jesus wants. In the dark days after his crucifixion, the crowds had gone, but the family, with only one exception, remained. And it was on the foundation of that family that, after Pentecost, he built his church.

Jesus was never tempted to play the numbers game. Matthew records a significant incident. He tells us that as soon as Jesus saw a crowd gathering, he "gave orders to go over to the other side" (Mt. 8:18). I wonder how many preachers today would make the choice Jesus did, to run in the other direction when he saw a massive number of potential church members heading his way!

It isn't that Jesus didn't care for the people or didn't want to reach them. Of course he did! It's that he knew the only way to reach them in the long run was by establishing a base of committed disciples who would multiply his own ministry in the world once he was gone. Otherwise all they would be left with was the memory of a massive signs and wonders movement based on the ministry of a man no now longer among them. Successful Christian leaders are always training others for the day they will no longer be there. That's why men like Calvin, Luther and Wesley left movements behind them. In our own day, it's why John

Wimber (see the chapter on healing) invested so much time training people in healing rather than just doing it himself. When he died, he left a movement behind him.

The crowds came and went and did their own thing. They were there for Jesus to meet their needs, and then they went home. But the disciples had no home to go to. Disciples are men and women committed to obeying their Master and Lord. Discipleship is unconditional. It is not telling God how or when or where we want to serve him. Discipleship is listening to God telling us how all those things are going to happen, whether it suits our preferences or not. So the question is — am I a disciple, or am I just another member of the crowd?

Back to Matthew's story. As Jesus was preparing to get into the boat, he was met by two men wanting to join his small band of disciples. If this was Jesus' church growth opportunity, he missed it. The first man, a scribe, announced his willingness to follow Jesus wherever he went (Mt. 8:19). The Jewish practice was for an individual to decide which Rabbi he wanted to follow. He was then free to do so, without any particular expectation in return. But Jesus, alone among all the Rabbis of Israel, took the opposite approach. He chose his followers. And then he truly discipled them. The scribe announced his willingness to follow Jesus wherever he went, but Jesus' reply to him ("The Son of Man has nowhere to lay his head") revealed his perception that the scribe did not really understand what discipleship was all about, and the scribe's subsequent silence verified that. This man wanted the blessing of being with Jesus, but without having to pay the price. A second candidate for discipleship approached, but immediately asked for a leave of absence (verse 21). He wanted to "bury his father" first. This was a Jewish expression for fulfilling a son's duty to look after his father for the remainder of his life. In other words, the request was to be a disciple, but later. Jesus confronted him with the statement that discipleship must take precedence over everything else.

Does this mean Jesus did not care about the crowds? Or that numbers meant nothing to him? Not at all. He laid down his life for every one of us. What it means is that the path to reaching the many is through disciples, not through the hangers-on. A megachurch built on the preacher's personality may produce nothing more than commitment a mile wide and an inch deep, and the church will disappear along with the preacher. A small church producing disciples will send them out to change nations.

If we turn away from discipleship, it's because we don't want to pay the cost. But the price is worth paying, and for this reason alone: *discipleship is the only way to draw close to Jesus.* The crowds were on the fringe of the meetings. The disciples were at the heart. Do you want to be close to him? Do you want to be the one close enough to touch the hem of his garment? Do you want to be close enough for him to touch you?

There's a simple answer. Become a disciple!

You'll never regret it.

IF YOU LOVE JESUS YOU LOVE HIS CHURCH

Peter had denied Jesus three times. When Jesus encountered him on the shores of the Sea of Galilee after his resurrection, he gave him three commands: feed my lambs; tend my sheep; and feed my sheep. Peter answered the first command with the words: "Yes, Lord; you know that I love you" (Jn. 21:15). When Jesus seemingly ignored his answer and persisted in his questioning, Peter was grieved. In the moment of his hurt, he failed to recognize the significance of what was happening. The threefold command was Peter's personal restoration after his threefold denial.

And in the process, Jesus was connecting the dots for Peter that would determine the course of the rest of his life. To love him was to love his church. Many years later, the man who witnessed this incident and wrote the story down would make the same point: "If anyone says, 'I love God,' and hates his brother, he is a liar; for he who does not love his brother whom he has seen cannot love God whom he has not seen. And this commandment we have from him: whoever loves God must also love his brother" (1 Jn. 4:20-21).

Cynicism is one of the most corrosive and dangerous things we can encounter. Cynicism about the church Jesus loves is a fire stoked by hell. The imperfections and failings of the church are only a function of the imperfections and failings of its members, including you and me. Just as we are called to love even our enemies, let alone our brothers and sisters, we are called to love the church.

There are many so-called churches which are nothing more than religious organizations. They have long since abandoned true loyalty to Christ. I am not speaking of those. Sometimes we do have to leave a local church and find a different fellowship, and there are all sorts of reasons why. But there is never any good reason to leave the church entirely.

When the Bible speaks of the church, it means the local church, not some mystical universal organization. The manifestation of the body of Christ in any given location is one of the many local churches we have access to. We can move from one to another, though only for good reason, but to leave commitment to any local church is to leave the church. Period. And that is sin. Sin that grieves the heart of the One who called us to follow him in laying down his life for that church.

My hope is in the words of Scripture, that Christ is returning for a bride holy and without blemish. That bride is the collection of local churches across the face of this earth. Churches for which he died and which he loves. That should be all the motivation we need to serve the church with our whole heart all the days of our lives, and so to be part of the bride for which he is coming.

Marana tha. Come, Lord Jesus.

ABOUT THE AUTHOR

From the Toronto region. David holds three degrees in theology. He and his wife, Elaine, have planted churches in the UK and Canada. David also teaches internationally in churches, Bible colleges, leadership training centers, and the online platforms TheosUniversity and TheosSeminary. David and Elaine have eight children and six grandchildren which, let's be honest, is an accomplishment.

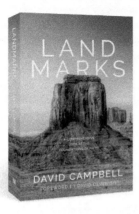

Landmarks
*A Comprehensive Look
at the Foundations of Faith*

By David Campbell

FIND THE WONDER IN HIS INCREDIBLE PLAN

Landmarks by David Campbell charts our course from the Word of God to our everyday lives. Each marker on this trail of bread crumbs reminds us of an essential truth that has shaped our knowledge of God and his plan. This is not a history book or an opinion piece; it's a compendium of foundational belief that celebrates monumental breakthroughs in christian understanding. Reading through Landmarks will leave you enlightened, grateful and strengthened in your faith.

Other titles by David Campbell

Mystery Explained
A Simple Guide to Revelation

By David Campbell

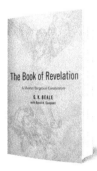

The Book of Revelation
A Shorter Exegetical Commentary

By G.K. Beale
With David Campbell

All titles available from Amazon
or from unprecedentedpress.com/shop

CPSIA information can be obtained
at www.ICGtesting.com
Printed in the USA
BVHW061524200223
658844BV00016B/1036